THE ART OF

INNER ALCHEMY

UNDERSTANDING THE PURPOSE OF THIS LIFE AND YOUR GROWTH WITHIN IT

KELLY SCHWEGEL

Cover artwork by Isabella Batten
Cover designed by Isabella Batten & Eli Wedel

Manufactured by Book Baby

Ordering information:
www.kellyschwegel.com
www.innerwisdomcircle.com

"Conjunction Junction" used by permission from
American Broadcasting Music, Inc. All rights
reserved.

ISBN: 978-1-48359-259-6

Acknowledgements

I would like to thank those who led to the unfolding of the content, building and possibility of this book.

To my amazing Guides who spoke these words so eloquently through me.

To my daughter Elisabeth Melcher for being my spiritual partner in this life, and standing by my side as I moved through these stages of alchemy with wisdom and grace.

To my parents, Joan and Stephen Schwegel, and sisters Kristin Zaal, Katrina Gongola and Kathleen Schwegel for helping to shape who I am, accepting who I have become and surviving my teen years.

To my editor, Elizabeth Rose, for her passion, compassion, intelligence and unconditional love.

To all of my clients and students who have allowed the beautiful messages of my Guides to touch their lives.

To all those who gave to me in selfless ways, and grew with me as I moved through the final stages of alchemy:

Dr. Russ L'HommeDieu	Dennis Mukai
Nia Peeples	Caity Fitzgerald
Catherine Coffey	Chau Mai
Doc and Carol Pierce	Karal Gregory
Jonathon Koharik	Janet Jamesson
Kevin Ceh	Felicia Maheux
The staff at the Heartmath Institute	Amber Cooney
	Captain Bryan Edward
Pamela Robbins	Linda Beach

Table of Contents

List of Figures

Preface

Baz Luhrmann said, "A life lived in fear is a life half lived." To me, a life half lived is no life at all. I was born with a purpose and drive to help change humanity that has not waivered since I had the consciousness to realize it. I am fiery and driven and have vehemently followed my inner voice and passions to make a difference my whole life, so to me, half living my passions would be painful.

Five years ago I was an educational trainer and developer for a state agency in Wisconsin. I was well known, successful and full of my own self-importance. So when I heard in meditation that I was going to give up my career as a trainer, which took me three degrees and thirteen grueling years of working in education to achieve, I laughed out loud. Five years later I can say that working in education feels like a lifetime ago and the last five years of working as a holistic healing practitioner has been gratefully humbling and is the world I now know and love.

Two weeks ago, I found myself asking what direction I was to take next in my healing life, with writing not one of my obvious options. I was living at the top of a mountain in California's Los Padres Mountains, away from commotion, electric lines, cell service, and, well, people. Moving there was my attempt to sit in my own silence and move away from distractions, healing from a brutal year of change and listening for my next steps in life. What I heard at the top of that mountain pushed me in a direction I never saw coming.

I am a clairvoyant, and I learned a long time ago never to make apologies for that. Frankly, I laugh when I say it, because, although I undeniably perceive things seemingly not of this reality, I am not your typical crystal ball psychic. I am what I playfully call a "conservative clairvoyant". To me, this is a non-mystical, shake no rattles, hold no ceremonies, type of person who also just happens to see auras, hear animals thoughts, speak to spirit Guides and knows things about people and the universe that I conceivably should not know. I suppose that being raised by two tea party republican, catholic, conservative parents might have had something to do with my being the pragmatic psychic I am. I can guarantee you that every time I gain some incredible intuitive insight about something in life, I hear my father's voice saying something doubtful and questioning. I love that. It keeps me real and grounded. It is because of Mr. Doubting Dad that I continuously seek scientific answers or biological reasoning to back up what I am intuitively learning from my Guides.

Yes, I speak with a set of Guides. And, yes, I am talking about the floating around without a body type of Guides. If it helps you, think of it like the guardian angel variety, kind of like It's a Wonderful Life's, Clarence Odbody, Angel 2nd Class. Yeah, I guess you can say it's like him, but without the bumbling stammer and badly tailored white dress. Well, that and my Guides do not appear to me in person, just perceptively through words and pictures shown through my mind's eye. I have been clairvoyant all of my life and started consciously speaking to one guide, my great grandmother Genevieve, when I was about eight. I am sure I listened to her earlier in life, I was just not aware that I was doing so. I remember the day

I consciously realized that someone was talking to me. In vain I tried telling my sisters that I *knew* things and I could hear someone telling me things. That was only to be received with a, "Liar, you do not!" response so I eventually just left it alone only to be known as my weird, secret, inner world.

I never met her, my great-grandmother Genevieve, since she died before I was born; but when I found a picture of her in my parent's attic, I knew she was the one who spoke to me. I actually remember her saying, quietly in my head the way she always spoke to me, *That's me*! when I found the picture. She was always there. Even through my angry teen years or my I-am-not-going-to-be-a-psychic thirties! Always constant, always guiding, always present. My youngest sister had invisible friends who she played with, but for me, it was just not a question of this being imaginary. Genevieve told me of things I could not possibly know. She told me about people: what they were like and, often times, secrets about them. Before age eight I believe I thought this was normal and everyone had this. You can imagine my confusion when I realized this was not other people's reality.

By the time I was nineteen I began receiving premonitions and seeing visions, which I also kept pretty quiet. I was an insecure teen and adding this weirdness to the pot of being me was not even on my radar to expose. These visions first came as a quick flash that was almost indiscernible, but they held a tremendous amount of information that I would receive instantaneously. I eventually learned to hold a flash in my mind's-eye and see it clearly while allowing my inner most being to process the information given. Now I see more than a quick flash, I actually see movie reels of people's lives with complete understanding of why they are being shown. Trust me when I say, this is very cool.

Probably my most memorable vision, and one of my first, was when I broke my vertebrae in 1988. In this instance, the visions started by my seeing a quick flash of an ambulance in my head. I remember questioning, *did I just see that*? For the next two weeks, these flashes of images of this ambulance began to stay longer and hold more information, kind of like they were building up a story within me. The last vision I had prior to my accident was of the ambulance, its doors closing and it driving away. I knew I was in it and I was badly hurt.

That same night my father was driving me to my boyfriend's house to go tobogganing. Now, if you're not from an It's-so-blasted-cold-I-cannot-blink-my-frozen-eyelashes climate, you may not know that a toboggan is a sled that holds four to five people on it. See, we in Wisconsin do more than tip cows for fun, we also pile multiple people onto big sleds and charge down snow-covered hills hoping no trees magically grew on the sled path overnight. On this night, on the car ride to the hill, I remember looking out the side window at the snow that had lightly begun falling. My mind was blank and really quite calm. In the midst of my silent mind I heard a beautiful, what I describe as silky, disembodied voice say, *Don't go, you're going to be hurt*. I don't remember ever hearing this voice. Not before and not since. I believe I was spoken to by a different kind of guide, an angel of protection. I remember knowing intuitively I needed to listen and said to my dad, "Dad, I can't go." He was quiet for an instant then said, "Why?" "I'm going to be hurt," came my very sheepish reply. He paused a little more and asked,

"How do you know that?" I knew I couldn't tell him what I had heard. I had witnessed him calling my mother a flake when she spoke of seeing auras, or knowing something she was clearly hearing intuitively and had made a conscious decision early on that I was not going to let him, or anyone else, know that I too was a flake. So instead of revealing this disembodied message, I answered, "I don't know, I just know." My father, a kind, loving man, is also very strong-minded and not someone you talk to about listening to other worldly warnings. He looked at me a bit strangely. "Well, don't go!" he said in an exasperated tone. I whined a little saying, "But I have a date." Having little patience for his four daughter's whines, he answered in an irritated, gruff voice, "Well, then go!" So I went.

Later that night, in the emergency room after learning that I had broken my vertebrae in two places, my dad asked me if I remembered what I had said to him. I had. It was one of those instances where I had not listened to my intuitive guidance and later wished I had. I have since learned to do as I am told or things will most definitely turn out hard. Trust me, I have tested those waters, not listening to the warnings, instructions or advice of my Guides, and trust me even more when I say, it is absolutely not worth the defiance. I clairvoyantly hear in those instances, *If you don't listen and move on your own, the universe will have to move you for you, and then it will be painful.* Yeah, I have learned to listen.

Interestingly, in line with my vision about the night of the back-breaking toboggan ride, I was unable to be taken via Flight for Life to the spinal cord injury unit because, as is typical for a Wisconsin winter, a blizzard had come in and the

13

helicopter was not an option. Consequently I had to be sedated and taken by ambulance, just as my vision had shown.

I have had many of these experiences in my life. Sometimes seeing premonitions of what was to come. Sometimes peering into my own body and speaking a deep truth about myself or my health. Often listening to instruction about this perceivably mystical life. And I am constantly peering into my client's bodies to see what they need to heal within themselves so that they may become healthier and happier. My intuitive abilities increase and change constantly and I am always in the process of learning something new from my incredible set of Guides.

About nine years ago my great grandmother guide turned into a group of Guides, who, as you can see, I respectfully, but without an ounce of creativity call, "My Guides." They are loving, inspirational, informational and, I say in all fondness, the equivalent of a really bossy parent. If you ever thought being scolded by a parent was bad, try an ethereal scolding. Now, don't get me wrong; they are never mean or unloving, and certainly not aggressive, but they do like to let me know when I cross the line with judgment, self-projection or any of those other human traits common to us mortal beings. It feels like a scolding from within the core of my being. My Guides' scolding, which can be more accurately described as calling me out on my humanness, is instantaneous and carries with it an internal knowing that I have just completely operated from a place of ego. I'd like to say I hate those scoldings, but I have to admit, I secretly love that they call me out on my shit.

My Guides are amazing. Now, at the age of forty-eight, I have a hard time putting into words the experiences I have; always blending this physical world with the ethereal. My Guides show me visions, explain the unknown, teach me about the mathematics of life, share with me universal knowledge, help me see what is needed to help people heal and speak right through me in the form of channeling. Regardless of all of this, I do not tell people what star system I come from, nor do I care. I do not obsess about my past lives; I live in this one. I bring though wisdom and knowledge, but swear like a trucker. I am no guru. I do not want to be one, but I respect and honor the information my Guides share, and I know that their teachings on how to heal have moved me from an unhappy, unhealthy person to a happy, healthy one. According to them, this book is about bringing that healing journey to you.

The Beginning

did not know I was writing this book. Two weeks prior to beginning this writing, I was preparing for teaching one of my online wisdom classes and, as I typically do, I asked my spirit Guides for inspiration for the hour-long class. They told me I would be writing about healing the physical body and directed me to go to my neighbor's home. Jonny is not really a neighbor in that neighborly sense of the word. Though his house is next to mine, it is a second home and in the last four months I had lived there, I had seen him visit only twice. The home is his sanctuary. Despite our lack of frequent contact, I'd been gifted a key and an open offer to enter this sacred space at any time.

And so, upon the direction of my Guides, enter I did. I took in the instantly calming, magnificent scene. A multitude of crystals were displayed, deliberately and delicately, around his home. Deeply expressive arrangements of his own creations adorned the walls, tables and floor. Even his furniture, many pieces in a purposefully tattered, exposed condition, told an artistic tale of the rich frailty of life. As I stood in a dreamy appreciation for what I like to think of as *Jonnyworld*, my Guides told me to take an alchemy book off of the library shelf. Jonny has a collection of books that would make Merlin himself jealous. Spiritual texts, sacred geometric teachings, inspiring reads about healing, a few about conspiracy and a lot about alchemy lined the shelves. Feeling into what book to take down, I instinctively grabbed <u>Alchemy Workbook</u> by Dennis William Hauck. It was at this point I seemed to go into autopilot mode, not consciously thinking, but for the duration of my stay, proceeded to absorb, analyze and organize nonetheless.

As I was directed, I sat down at Jonny's kitchen table with the alchemy book to my left and my computer to my right. I was staring at an antique picture frame on the wall to the left of me, free from any glass or backing, that framed a pair of worn ballet shoes. Those tranquil pink shoes triggered a warm, gentle feeling within me and I instinctively closed my eyes. As I was taught by my Guides to do years ago, I drifted my conscious thought back from the front of my head to the center of my head and opened up to that place in my consciousness where I am at complete peace. The place where they can speak and be heard. The place where I see, hear, perceive, understand, feel, and know instantaneously. The place of color, vibration, and vastness. It is this place inside me where my Guides bring their voice, through my being, to be heard and known. All went still. At this moment I began to hear a low, deep pulsing hum coming from inside of my head. *This is not typical*, was my momentary understanding. By the third pulsing sound, my sight went red. I believe I opened my eyes at this point. The red was still there for a moment and as my sight came back into clarity. I saw a mercury colored orb, about two inches in diameter, floating above the left page of the opened alchemy book and intuitively heard, *I am with you*.

Instead of having any conscious thought about how atypical this experience was for me, I obsessively delved into the alchemy book and started creating a PowerPoint of what I was absorbing. Slide after slide of the breakdown of the seven stages of the alchemical process sprang forth from me. Endless slides captured transforming physical matter, our mental & emotional state and our physical state, from the impure and imbalanced into something pure and balanced. I documented how the alchemical process relates to our transforming our soul into something wiser. I put aside information no longer relevant and clarified information that was misinterpreted; and I added, through the wisdom of these voices within me, so much more to the process of healing our ego selves and the physical body than what I read in the book. I recall internally asking why this new information was being brought forward now, since The Emerald Tablet—the reputed backbone and historical document of alchemical studies—has been around for over 2000 years. My Guides explained to me that the world at that time was not ready to understand and accomplish what humanity is ready for now, especially where healing the physical body is concerned. I accepted this and continued to absorb the eerily familiar process of alchemy.

When I had finished writing about and interpreting the last stage, Coagulation, I sat upright staring at what my Guides and I had created and realized what this was. They had just brought through me the understanding of my life. I then experienced a very quick, but very thorough life review of my healing my body of nine different physical conditions. Quick flashes of moments of my life shuffled through my mind as they also showed me healing my emotional body of worthlessness, shame, guilt, fear, anger and resentment, and then of healing my mind of chatter full of doubt and insecurity. They also flashed pictures of me conducting over a thousand sessions helping others to do the same. With my mind completely blown, my Guides said to me, *You are the alchemist.* I was stunned. I saw more flashes of my life as I broke down and sobbed. I was sobbing because I instantly knew what my life here was all about; to go through the process of healing myself so that I could first-hand understand the painful, incredible, gut-wrenching, beautiful process of alchemical healing. It is then that I could bring that understanding to others.

I do not know how long I sat there, heart thumping and stunned, but eventually my Guides told me that I would be writing a book about my life of alchemizing my mind, emotions, physical body and my soul. They showed me the pages in the book and an instant understanding of each of the chapters.; and they explained to me that the information would come through me effortlessly.

I do not remember packing up my computer or putting the alchemy book back on Jonny's shelf, but I found myself walking back to my place without thought. Maybe I was touching the ground as I walked or maybe not; all I remember is that I was in a dream-like state and the mountains surrounding me seemed far away, yet inseparable from me.

I walked in my front door and my friend Karal, who had been staying with me for a couple of days said, in the most fondly memorable Virginian drawl, "Well, either you just saw a ghost or a bear and I honestly do not know which one that would be!" I tried speaking, but could not form anything coherent and soon broke down and sobbed again. Poor Karal must have felt completely helpless as I finally half cried and half spoke out what had happened. At the end, she just stared at me and said, "You know it's only been 30 minutes since you left, don't you?"

I still do not know how that is possible, but it happened. I had absorbed the alchemical book, made changes, added clarity to the alchemical stages, created a PowerPoint about it, went through a life review and a vision about this book in 30 minutes. We can get into any number of conversations at this point about time warps, other dimensions, or other supernatural explanations, but to be honest, I just care that it happened.

Introduction
Alchemy
Making the impure, pure

Come to your own realization of what is and what is not...seriously, you're not a sheep

Alchemy: The word is derived from the Arabian phrase "al-khemia," which...just kidding, we are not going to get that technical in this book. The process of alchemy can be a very serious, very deep and very spiritual practice that alchemists spend much of their lives perfecting and understanding. I, however, was not brought down this long path to understanding or experiencing alchemy. As I previously shared in the preface, my alchemical education consisted of living an agonizing forty-eight year process of alchemizing my mind, body and soul, followed by receiving a 30-minute tutorial from my Guides of the seven stage process of alchemy and how it relates to everything we experience in this life. I have no authority to speak "technically" about alchemy, but am honored to share the term and its seven stages to help you understand the process of internal healing and growing, and, of course, the meaning of life.

Alchemy is described as the purification of metals, substances, the mind, the physical body, and the soul. Basically, it is making the impure, pure. It is said to be the secret of nature and is said to be able to perfect anything. Yes, that means even you. It doesn't matter how messed up you think your emotions are, how far down the rabbit hole your chatter-mind has traveled or how sick and diseased your body is. By understanding the purpose of this world we live in and understanding the alchemical process, you will heal and grow to one degree or another in this lifetime. The more you understand and engage in these stages of alchemy, the more pure you will become as a soul and a human.

The study of alchemy can be traced back thousands of years to the Indian Vedic Texts, the Chinese Chin, the Islamic Rasayana and to the first day of creation by Judaic alchemists. Greek philosophers describe alchemy as applying to all matter and teach of it in nature and the Egyptians made it a science. (Latz, 1995) Healing our beingness—yes, I think I made that word up to mean human and soul existence—is not new and the process has not changed much in over 2000 years. This book is now being written to make the understanding of alchemical healing easy to digest and motivate you to either venture into that healing process or acknowledge and further the wonderful work you may have already begun.

You will find that many alchemists encourage that this work always be part of a personal, spiritual practice and that getting into a solemn meditative state should occur before engaging in any alchemical work. I have found that, although I engage in formal meditation here and there, I do not engage in a regular spiritual practice. I do not feel that I am disrespectful of the alchemical method or of my healing process if I am not. I simply live my life through the wisdom of my Guides, continuously seeking answers and insight from within. I have learned, for the most part, to stay out of mind-chatter and be open to receive readily. Although I take time continuously throughout the day to clear my body of negativity and quiet my mind, I am usually not making any formal affair of it; chanting Om or sitting cross-legged in a surreal sunset. I am human and from time to time get irritated, react, and sometimes have the desire to judge, but that never lasts long. I just move into my compassion and understanding of life and all negative human reaction fades quickly. I live a pretty normal life, just with Source as my constant companion. So that you are clear, source, to me, can be considered God energy, love energy, or a consciousness that embodies all that is. What Source is called doesn't matter to me, it just matters to me that its beautiful, unconditioned energy is constantly present and flowing through me.

As you absorb the material in this book, and go through your personal process of inner growth, decide for yourself whether you want to grow with ceremony, rituals or a spiritual practice, or without. That is up to you. As you read about my story and this process, I encourage you to listen to the prompts from within. Listen to your own inner voice, and if it says meditate, go meditate. If it says get into a disciplined spiritual practice, then do so. We are all so vastly unique in our journeys here and it is important to honor and recognize our different approaches as perfect, despite how different they may be from one another. Feel what is right for you. In other words, come to your own realization of what is and what is not...seriously, you're not a sheep.

My Guides have told me that now is the time for humanity to bridge the gap between the mystical view and the scientific view of healing and personal growth. The timeliness of this book is divine and if you are reading this, it is divine timing for your growth and healing as well. So, are you ready? Let's begin to bridge that gap and expand your soul by talking alchemy. Here are the seven stages of alchemy in their basic understanding.

Stage 1: **Calcination** – To convert with heat or burning
Stage 2: **Dissolution** – To undo or break down
Stage 3: **Separation** – Breaking apart or letting go
Stage 4: **Conjunction** – Union
Stage 5: **Fermentation** – Change
Stage 6: **Distillation** – Purification
Stage 7: **Coagulation** – To change into a thicker, stronger mass

We are going to examine each of these stages in detail, but if you take a look at the process in general and think of any massive internal growth or healing you've had, you may be able to see your healing process within these stages. If not, hold on to your hat because we are about to go on an alchemical ride of learning how to make the impure, pure; how to make you a stronger, deeper, more healed you.

What is a Soul?

Many describe a soul as the immortal essence of a being. I agree with this, and I also describe it as existing as conscious energy. The soul is a conscious awareness that is not confined to a physical body. This conscious awareness has a unique set of wisdom to it, and it is simultaneously connected to a unified conscious whole. This "whole" can be described as universal consciousness that all souls share and are connected to energetically. Your soul, or your conscious energy, is not confined to a particular gender, a specific space, or time. It grows in its wisdom and expands in its capacity to exist as unconditional love

Before we go any further, I need to explain that after processing what I learned about the stages of alchemy during my Jonnyworld experience, explained in the introduction, I was struck with a quandary. I was shown how my healing my mental body, my emotional body, my physical body, and consequently my soul body, followed the stages of the alchemical process. However, I was struck by how often I realized I had been through these stages again and again throughout my life. It seemed that I was not brought through this process once, but many times. Well, this left me completely confused so I promptly asked my Guides for clarification.

What they explained is that you will go through experiencing learning around and completion of these alchemical stages at a macro level, which is your overall growth as a soul. And you will also go through experiencing learning around and completion of them at a micro level, which is your learning a karmic life lesson here on Earth. A karmic life lesson is a lesson you learn about yourself, life, and existence so that you can expand in your wisdom and unconditional love as a person and consequently as a soul.

My Guides said that you are actually going through all of these alchemical stages simultaneously, on both the macro and micro levels. You are always taking small steps toward learning about each of them, but you will not complete an alchemical stage at the macro soul level until you have learned all of the micro karmic lessons needed to achieve it. To learn a micro karmic lesson you will keep experiencing the good, bad, beautiful and ugly behaviors, feelings and emotions around different life lessons until you have gained the necessary wisdom to completely understand it.

Your soul goes on a long journey of healing and growing and due to the vast number of different life lessons you need to learn, therefore you will go through many different lifetimes to learn them. You do this until you complete all of the lessons there are to learn about living with the Ego here on Earth. By doing this you will further expand your soul consequently moving through the stages of alchemizing the soul as a whole.

This might sound overwhelming, but do not let that affect your moving into your own personal growth. Saying that there are many lifetimes of healing to come may cause you to say, "Well, why try to heal things now if I have so many lifetimes of growth and healing to come! What's the point?" The point is that yes, we are on a long journey of growing, but by understanding the purpose of our growth and why we move into sadness, pain, suffering, heartache or loss, it all becomes much easier to move through. Moving through growth and healing at any level will make your current reality a more positive and healthy one for you to exist within.

Here is where I make my big disclaimer; I am not trying to convince you of anything, change your religious beliefs or ask you to join me in a belief system that does not resonate with you. I am not a cult leader, nor do I believe in gurus. I am going to present the understandings I have gained through the experiences of listening to my Guides throughout my lifetime, and other people's Guides during the thousand plus personal healing sessions I have delivered. I ask only that you listen to what you believe inside of you. Listen to what resonates with you, and make your own determination as to the rightness or wrongness of these messages for you and your beliefs. Listen inside of you and make your own determination as to what you believe to be true. Ok, now that that is out of the way, I shall continue.

In some of your lifetimes you may only experience the completion of stage one of alchemy while others may bring about the completion of multiple stages. This all depends on where you are at in your karmic learning. Each lifetime of learning is cumulative and, again, although you are always learning all of the alchemical stages simultaneously, you can only reach the completion of a stage once you have gained all of the wisdom necessary to expand fully into that stage.

Think of it like this, you have most likely been receiving instruction about science all of your life, either formally or informally. You would have been learning about the principles of, let's say, physics since you were a young child; it just would

29

have been explained to you in a very basic manner. As you age, mature and gain more knowledge you would then engage in more complex learning around it, little by little. By the time you are ready to learn the complexities of physics you would have already gained the background knowledge needed to receive the new, more complex material and understand it. In other words, you would be able to pass a formal physics class because you had gained all of the necessary knowledge needed to prepare you for your big learning around that subject.

This is much like how you progress through your stages of alchemy. You are constantly being presented with lessons that are bringing you closer and closer to completing a stage of alchemical growth. You are going through overall macro alchemical growth as a soul, but while here on Earth you experience different lifetimes of learning that allows you to progress through the micro alchemical growth as a human. Because of the uniqueness of each soul, some souls learn fast, others more slowly, so some take more lifetimes to progress in their karmic learning than others. Every soul is different.

So, the question you may have at this point is, "Why are we going through this process of learning, alchemizing and gaining all of this wisdom? To what end? To explain this better, I need to explain the purpose of life. Yes, I am going to explain that with a straight face, and no, it is not the number 42 as Douglas Adams painstakingly reveals in "The Hitchhiker's Guide to the Universe."

Life here on Earth is nothing but a big classroom for your soul. Your soul actually ages, just as your body does. It ages from baby, to infant, to young, to mature to old like your body, except your body ages through time and your soul ages through wisdom gained through multiple lifetimes. This includes lifetimes of learning by making mistakes, doing positive things and negative things, laughing, loving, hurting and harming.

My Guides have explained that to gain wisdom we have to go through the yin and yang of everything life has to offer. Through many different lifetimes we would have been male and female, rich and poor, the victim and the perpetrator, the murderer and the murdered, the pedophile and the molested, gay and straight, famous and a recluse, and on and on. I remember when my Guides were first teaching me about this I self-righteously said to myself, *I am sure I have never murdered before.* Ha! Big mistake on my part. Later that week I was walking down the street, thinking nothing in particular, when I was stopped in my tracks. I was suddenly blasted with the feelings of me as a murderer. I felt the motivation, the **emotional state I was in**, the adrenaline coursing through my body, and my mental state desiring power right before I murdered. Thank God I was not shown the actual act, but at that moment I knew that in another lifetime I had murdered. I intuitively understood that in that lifetime I was powerful and male and I wanted to protect my fortune and power at any cost, and therefore murdered. I was stunned. I angrily asked my Guides, *What was that! Why did you show me that?* and they lovingly, yet firmly stated to me, *Kelly, do not think for one second that you have not done something of this nature. You cannot get to this stage of soul development and not have done "wrong" things in your lifetimes. Of course you have. It is part of the balance of the universe and part of the learning every soul goes through to understand both sides of everything. That balance*

31

gives you wisdom and that wisdom expands your ability to love unconditionally. They further explained that I could not possibly work well with other people in healing situations if I did not understand that there really is no right or wrong in the eyes of Source. Yes, I realize this is a controversial statement. No, I do not believe in or like murdering. Yes, I do believe we should not do it, and yes, I agree with accountability for those actions. However, I also believe that for us to know true love and wisdom, during one lifetime or another, our journey is to learn the opposite of love along with learning about love itself. It is through these lifetimes that we not only teach others so much, but we deepen our internal understanding of all of life allowing us to gain a balanced wisdom that otherwise could never be learned.

After that vision of my murderous past life, I felt inside of me that I could never have understood what it felt like to have murdered if I had not experienced it first hand. I could not have read about that in a book, seen it in a move or been told about it to understand so intimately how that felt. I felt the balance of knowing intimately the difference between saving someone and ending their life. I saw the wisdom in the experience and at a core level agree with this you-have-to-experience-it-to-understand-it method of teaching & learning as a soul.

Another example that really nails the idea of experiencing the yin and yang, or opposites, of everything came through when I was mentoring a student of mine. She was sharing with me that she had a vision of a past life of hers where she was a six-year-old girl in the Holocaust. She went on to explain that she knew that in that lifetime she was put to death in the gas chambers. I then shared that I too had a past life where I was a part of the Holocaust. I was a nineteen-year-old male, I was German and I was the one who did the gassing. She was stunned. She stared at me with astonished eyes as she slowly said, "Wow. So in that lifetime you put me to sleep, but in this lifetime you woke me up." Then it was my turn to be stunned. Yes, I knew that to be truth. The horrendous deeds I engaged in during my past lives gave me balance of wisdom, which now allows me to assist others to awaken to their authentic, beautiful selves in this lifetime. This wisdom allows me to see that all souls are beautiful regardless of whatever it is they engage in during their lifetimes – right or wrong - and gives me a tremendous level of internal compassion for each soul living a human life. No, I don't like murderers. I'm not going to invite them over for a cold beer and a barbecue. But at the same time, I am not going to judge them either. They chose a very hard experience in that life and I can have compassion for that soul's lesson. Our souls learn of being kind, loving and compassionate souls by engaging in and understanding both sides of our human behavior, light and dark, positive and negative.

I have been challenged time and again on this understanding that we came here to Earth to purposefully engage in the good, bad, beautiful and ugly. That we knew that suffering, hardship, good and bad deeds, wounding and heartache are all part of this experience. And we gladly incarnate into a body to experience it. I actually had a gentleman say to me in a workshop once, "So, you are trying to tell me that children's suffering is for a higher purpose? That a loving God understands this?" "Yes." I answered. "I am."

33

My Guides explain this by first drawing a parallel between our soul opposites—perceived good versus bad—and Newton's third law of physics. This law states that for every action there is an equal and opposite reaction. A force is needed for this law to enact. Forces result from interactions, where some forces react from normal friction, tension or applied force and others are a result of distance interactions like gravitational, electrical and magnetic forces. Your soul is a force and a force always comes in pairs; equal and opposite action-reaction force pairs. Ok...in English you ask? Yes, here it is in as plain of language as I can give. Your soul is an energetic force of nature and it has two parts creating a friction between above (Source) and below (Earth). This experience here on Earth is to bring balance between both by learning to live as a beautiful, wise soul from Source, also known as heaven, while living in an ego-bound body here on Earth.

My Guides said to think of your soul as a pendulum. Swinging over to one side is pure, innocent, inexperienced love and the other side is the ego that wants to have self-importance and keeps you looking for love and acceptance from others. They said that we are swinging from innocent, unwise love over to the human conditions of the ego so that we can land in the center as a balanced, expansive, wise, unconditional loving being (see figure 1). I get asked all of the time what is so wrong with just being innocent love? Why wouldn't we just stay there? Well, pure, innocent love is unbalanced in that there is no experience or depth to it. It is not wise, expansive love. You could consider it fairy love or the love that comes in an innocent child. On the opposite end, the ego is all about materialism, wealth, status and power and the need for you to find love and acceptance through others instead of from within. It is fueled by the human condition and it promotes a constant strive for importance and specialness. Neither end of this pendulum is balanced, but if the innocent love-soul can move into the human conditioned ego-soul to find love THROUGH the ego experiences of hardship, challenges, fear, etc., it can swing to center and exist as wise, deep, healthy unconditional love because it has experienced life's conditioning. How can you exist in and understand unconditional love if you've never been conditioned?

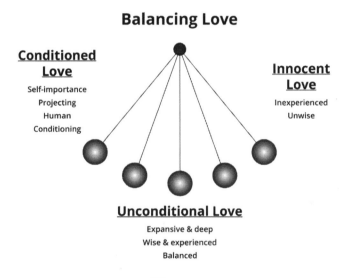

Balancing Love

Conditioned Love

Self-importance
Projecting
Human
Conditioning

Innocent Love

Inexperienced
Unwise

Unconditional Love

Expansive & deep
Wise & experienced
Balanced

Figure 1

Our soul is here on Earth learning about the ego in a safe manner in that no matter what you do to the physical body, you cannot kill your soul. You can harm this physical body in any number of unimaginable ways, but your soul will live on. You can incarnate into a body for as many lifetimes as is needed so that you gain the wisdom you need to be in balance as authentic, expansive, unconditional love that can operate with an ego and still be loving and kind.

Ok, now that you completely understand the meaning of life...back to the ages of souls. As I said, we go from baby, to infant, to young to mature, to old soul, aging through lessons learned, or wisdom gained. We live many lives and come here knowing each time what our major lessons are going to be. We choose our families, both positive and negative influential people to play roles in our karma, key situations and key events that will assist us in our karmic learning. For those of you who are visually minded, it might help to take a look at this graphic representing the ages of souls (see figure 2).

Soul's Earth Ages

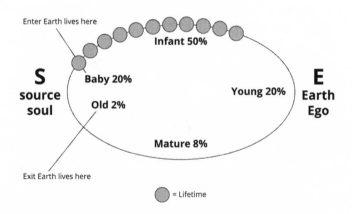

Figure 2

This graphic representation of soul's earth ages is linear due to our experiencing time here on earth; however, my Guides have indicated that we are actually experiencing all ages at the same time. Having just dropped that bomb, try not to let your mind wrap itself around this concept too much. It is somewhat inconsequential since we are currently in the reality of time-based existence. This concept tends to send people into a tailspin of mind-blowing chaos that in the end will just leave you with a pulsing headache. Let's just leave this discussion to the brilliant folks in the fields of psychology and neuroscience.

Looking at figure 2, the "S" equals soul or Source, meaning you are either fresh from Source existence or are about to enter back into it as a wise old soul. The "E" equals Earth or Ego, meaning you are completely Earth bound with materialism, wealth, status, power, money and ego. You travel clockwise around this chart from baby, to infant, to young, to mature, to old and then this Earth learning is done.

Yes, I realize that this probably triggered the question, "Well, then what?" In short, I will say that our soul goes through twelve levels of learning and this Earth school is only at level three, moving toward four. Now, this concept of overall soul stages and our moving toward four is another book entirely, but to appease your curiosity, see figure 3 outlining the different levels of overall soul development.

Now, back to the Earth Soul Age graphic (see figure 2). The percentages indicate the amount of people on the Earth who are currently in each category at this time. These percentages are in the process of changing, but that too is an entirely different book.

Levels of Overall Soul Development

Your soul continuously becomes more wise and expansive as you learn through the different experiences of your conscious energy. Earth existence is at level three, moving toward level four. Since everything consists of mathematics in the form of creation, movement, electricity and magnetism there are many levels of embodiment that you will go through to be at your most expanded, wise conscious level. These levels of soul development outline the progression of that conscious learning.

Level One-Creation of your soul
Level Two-Living physically through Instinct
Level Three-Living physically under the control of the ego
Level Four-Living physically with a tamed ego
Level Five-Soul experience as balanced, wise, unconditional love
Level Six- Gaining understanding of the universal laws and functions of nature and existence
Level Seven-Physically experiencing the different movements of a vortex
Level Eight-Existing physically as a planet, ocean, plant kingdom, etc.
Level Nine-Embodying a solar system
Level Ten-Embodying a universe
Level Eleven-Embodying above and below together (planet and source, Earth and Heaven)
Level Twelve-Embodying all that is

Figure 3

When my Guides first brought this soul-age chart through me (figure 2), I was sitting with a client in a session. I don't remember what it was she had asked me, but I immediately grabbed a clipboard of paper and drew out the soul age graphic. With authority, I explained it and all of the characteristics of the ages. At the time, I was out of my body listening from the background to my Guides explaining this concept. They were speaking through my mouth, but I was consciously listening. I remember saying to myself, as I heard myself talking, *This is so Fuc^*#ng cool! I am totally stealing this*! I was so excited because it explained so much about the people I had met in my life. Everyone I had met could easily be identified as one of these ages. I have used this graphic and explanation time and again to help people to understand and have compassion for themselves and for those who show up in their life.

Before you read through the following Earth's soul age descriptions, please keep in mind that this is not a hierarchy or a way to enforce your ego. The ego wanting to be important can easily cause someone to condescendingly think, *Well, I'm an old soul and you, baby soul below me, are not as good as I.* I like to refer to that as being in spiritual superiority, which, frankly, is nothing more than ego exemplified. Spiritual superiority is really just a neon sign saying, "Hi! I don't realize that I AM love, so I am looking for love, acceptance and approval from you. Therefore, I'm using my spiritual knowledge to look better than you while I put an *I am love* vibe on it so we both think I am not flawed." We are all human and we are all flawed. Each stage of soul development has different challenges and growth gained from it. They are not better than or worse than one another, they are just different. Think of it this way: just like you would never look at a three-year old in our society and say, "Oh my god! I can't believe you're three. I am clearly so much better than you are!" you wouldn't look at the age of a soul any different. If you catch yourself in spiritual superiority, you do not need to give yourself a shame-on-you time out, it is just a sign to take a look within and speak a genuine truth to yourself about your own self-love. If you truly realize that you ARE love, and are not looking for it outside of yourself, you would never care to put yourself above anyone else or view it from that standpoint.

Comparison is a slippery slope that leads to self-judgment, judgment of others and keeps the ego intact.

The wisdom gained increases with each lifetime lived so there is not a black and white line between each age. Your soul gets progressively wiser and more expansive in its ability to exist as unconditional love the more you progress through the ages. A soul at the beginning of the infant stage is quite different than a soul at the end of that age.

Also, please know that at each soul-age, there are mature and old souls present in each societal group or human experience. This is to help those at that particular soul level to grow; so do not think, for example, *Well, if I'm in a gang or fundamental religion then I must be a baby soul.* Remember, our journeys are all so vastly unique to our individual soul needs; there is no cookie-cutter way of defining how a person's journey should look and no black and white prescription for movement through these ages.

It is not important that you know your specific Earth soul age, but it is important to have compassion and tolerance for where anyone is at in their own soul development. Just as you would not look at that three-year-old child in our society and think you are better than them, you would also not say, "I need you to grow up right now and not cry because you're tired! I need you to fix your own food and drive a car because I expect you to be like me!" You do not expect a baby or infant soul to be a mature or old soul if they are not ready. Love others where they are at, and have compassion for the experiences they are learning at each stage of development, even if they collide with your journey and punch you in the gut, literally or figuratively. Accept they are where they are at because they are only reflecting the amount of wisdom, or lack of wisdom, they have gained in their soul's progression.

One last piece of understanding to have before you explore the different soul ages is that all souls have an energetic signature. What this means is that our souls and our bodies vibrate. All molecules in the body vibrate, move and radiate light at a rate that is unique to that soul, or person. Less wise souls will vibrate at a lower rate and souls with more wisdom will vibrate at a higher rate. This is, again, due to the amount of learning and experience they have achieved throughout their different lifetimes. For a good understanding of this, view Dr. David R. Hawkins' map of the levels of human consciousness in his book, Power vs. Force, or view the Energetic Signature chart that I adapted from his original chart (see figure 4).

Emotional States of Being Vibrational Scale

Modified from Dr. David R. Hawkins' Levels of Human Consciousness (2002)

Driver	Emotion/ Feeling	Scale	Description
Free of the ego	Pure Unconditional Love	700+	Conscious state of existence free of the ego and the human condition
Operating with tamed ego	Peace	600	Finding things to be perfect in their current state of existence
	Joy	540	Operating in an elevated state without care for what anyone else thinks
	Love	500	Operating AS love
Opening to your divinity	Wisdom	400	Open to communication from higher self & Guides. Tap into universal wisdom
	Acceptance	350	Accept that you are a beautiful being
Learning to love yourself	Willingness	310	Willing to see that the human condition is not permanent
	Surrender	250	Fall into a neutral state of being while you surrender into releasing old beliefs of the ego
	Courage	200	Courage to see this life as a classroom for your soul to grow and expand through the human experience
Surrendering into the ego	Pride	175	Feeling self-righteous in the attainment of self-importance through the eyes of others
	Anger	150	Either projection of hurt onto others or feeling you don't deserve to be treated a particular way
Fear	Desire	125	Fear of not being enough without material possessions or approval
	Sadness	75	Fear that you are in a hopeless state of low vibration, you are stuck or you are in a deep grief
	Apathy	50	Fear overtakes you causing you to shut down, moving you into a state of unfeeling, unmotivated, lack of passion
	Guilt	30	Fear you are not a good person. Feeling that you have not done the right thing or behaved in the right way
	Shame	20	Fear you are not enough. Feeling less than, or bad about who you are

Figure 4

42

Soul Ages

Baby Soul
The baby soul is fresh from Source, with little
wisdom gained. They have had few experiences
with ego lives and therefore do not know how to
handle mental or emotional challenges very well.
Due to this there is a lot of strife in their lives, or a
lot of *I'm gonna kick your ass* and *I hate you*
mentality. There is a tendency to disown people
and exhibit animalistic reactions, threats, violence
and much confusion as to how to handle life.
Please understand that amongst all of this there is,
of course, love, caring and kindness, but it is of a
different flavor than the older soul. There is
innocence to the love, almost blind love, and
desperation to receive love back. Their love is so
situated in need that when you reject or hurt them
they retaliate harshly. The baby soul is used to
existing in oneness due to being so fresh from
Source. In Source energy we all share access to a
universal consciousness so we never feel alone or
unsupported in our being. We feel universal love
and existence as a synchronized energy as
opposed to being separate, individual, ego-driven
beings like we are here on Earth. Because of this,
the baby soul gravitates to things like fundamental
religions, cults, warring religions, gangs, or they
have a massive need for family, group, state or
country belonging in search of that oneness. I refer
to that as the "Close the borders!" mentality. In
addition, to gain the wisdom they need, fear-based
experiences like a fearful God or fear of society,
government or each other are necessary to keep
them learning at their stage of development. Baby
souls are also so far from Earth energy that they do
not know how to manifest money yet, so typically
struggle financially. They are usually stuck in
poverty, feeling a victim to the economy or their

financial situation. They are happiest when they are supported by their family, country, tribe or group.

Infant Soul

Infant souls are half way between Source energy and Earth energy. They have gained more wisdom so exist in what I describe as emotional and mental strife with etiquette. They are not going to *kick your ass* because that is unacceptable behavior, but they tend to gossip behind your back, judge, be self-righteous or have an indignant attitude. They believe that there is an expected way of behaving and all should conform to that. "I am normal!" is their motto. If you show up as different, it makes them very uncomfortable. They are happy to conform to the norms of their tribe, group or society and seldom rock the boat so as to look as "normal" as possible. They no longer need fundamental ways of being spiritual so are involved in less structured religions. They believe in politics, rules, the white picket fence and have an average standard of living. They are typically average income within their culture and work hard for their day's wage. They are happiest when their family is happy, their children are successful and life is going according to plan.

Young Soul

Young souls are completely immersed the in Earth energies of wealth, status, power and importance. They look to be in control and to be seen as better than others in society. They need "that car" "that house" "that relationship" or "that body" to feel good. They are so Earth bound that they know how to get the money and keep it from you. They do not prescribe to a religion with conviction and are often atheist. They need proof, the science or tangible evidence to believe something. Career

44

and achievement are very important to them due to being completely immersed in Earthly separateness from Source; it is about the individual and the individual's achievements at this stage. This age is all about the self and they are often narcissistic in nature. They will often throw others under the bus to look better, obtain power and control or achieve. They are happiest when others appreciate their skill, talents, achievements or social status.

Mature Soul

The mature souls have gained a significant amount of wisdom and experience. They begin to look at life from a different angle. Because they are ready to understand and move beyond fear-based thinking, doubt and the ego-bound personality, the veils of this life begin to unravel. They move into an understanding that this life is not about what you achieve, what educational degrees you have, how much money you have or your status in society. They internally know and accept that this life is a classroom for your soul, and they are learning to value their lessons, even when it is hard. This is the stage where souls learn to understand that it is fruitless to try to find love and acceptance outside of yourself, because that love and acceptance is already inside of them, the very fabric of who they are. They learn genuine self-love and do not care anymore whether people see them as "normal" or fitting in. They move to the beat of their own drum. In this stage, they learn that money is just life-force energy and can be manifested once they are in a healthy, loving space within. They want money to be peaceful and happy, but the motivation is different than that of the young soul's need to have money to be seen as success. They learn that they are beautiful, divine souls who are having a human experience to expand and deepen their love through wisdom gained. They go through an, often difficult, phase of shedding the ego, integrating all of their lessons and moving into a state of living life through a tamed ego. They are happiest when they are in a balanced state within, doing what they love and feeling passion and inspiration in their life.

Old Souls
Old souls are born into this life with vast wisdom. They have an innate sense of purpose that drives them since birth. They seem to naturally know about the wisdom of life without being externally taught. They are our wisdom teachers—those who are here to spread their knowledge humbly and without fanfare. They have the ability to tap into universal knowledge and often bring about significant understandings of life, spirituality, scientific advancements, creative inspiration and healing, and motivating art. They often have an internally balanced presence about them. They are very powerful in their internal energy, which radiates far and wide. Because of this powerful, radiant energy, people are either completely drawn to them or completely repelled by them, depending on what level that individual person is vibrating at. They love humanity deeply and often seek to bring about profound changes while here. They are happiest when they can operate free of the constraints of the ego and fulfill their purpose here with modesty.

Moving through these Earth soul ages, my beautiful readers, is alchemizing the soul at the third level of overall soul development. These Earth soul ages are all very necessary and cannot be skipped; we have to experience them all. Just as we cannot skip a physical age in this lifetime, we cannot skip a soul age throughout our lifetimes.

We do not get to check out of our learning our lessons. There are no CliffsNotes to just get the summary of our lessons, just as there is no *Purpose of Life for Dummies* book available. You need to move through the complete boxed set of the whole Earth's soul age series. I am often asked to communicate with those who are deceased for insight or healing for a client and several times I have communicated with those who have ended their own lives. I find it interesting what they consistently tell me, which is, *You do not get to check out of your lessons on Earth. If you end your life prematurely, you have to incarnate back into another body and do it all over again.*

The following chapters are all about healing through the stages of alchemy, which are played out within these stages of soul development, each micro karmic lesson and also in your macro overall soul development. Sharing of the alchemical stages is intended to open your awareness further about your purpose here and what you need to do to heal into internal love and self-acceptance by taming the self-important ego. Read and understand them with gentle compassion for the experiences you have had, and how even the most difficult of experiences is all for your greatest soul growth.

Chapter One
Calcination

To convert with heat or burning

*You did not come to Earth to be in peace; if
you were going to do that you would have
stayed where you were*

Reminder of the Alchemical Stages
Stage 1: Calcination:
To convert with heat or burning (human conditioning)
Stage 2: Dissolution:
To undo or break down (heal internal wounding)
Stage 3: Separation:
Breaking apart or letting go (see the ego when it shows up)
Stage 4: Conjunction:
Union (balance your opposites)
Stage 5: Fermentation:
Change (Dark night of your soul and golden light)
Stage 6: Distillation:
Purification (let go of old habits and safety zones)
Stage 7: Coagulation:
To change into a thicker, stronger mass

Calcination is stage one in any process of alchemy.
In this stage, whatever is being alchemized is
returned to its most fundamental ingredients so
that falsity can be removed. This is done through
the heating of a substance in an intense flame, or
burning it, until all that is left is a pile of white
ashes. The ashes are then pulverized, often using a
mortar and pestle and then heated over an open
flame in a crucible. When an alchemist is creating
an essential oil or transforming one metal to
another, they burn the animal, plant matter or

49

metal so that it is reduced to ash or bone and then pulverize it and heat it again.

Well, isn't this life? We get burned, pulverized, and then burned again until we are broken down into a pile of ashes. We develop insecurity, self-doubt, resentment, shame, guilt, fear, anger, and often times, anxiety and depression. This is called being conditioned by life, or human conditioning. The first part of your life is all about the Calcination stage of alchemy, getting burned enough by life so that you develop the perfect human conditioning to plunge you into internal change and growth. Seriously, in life you know that you have all kinds of positive, fun, peaceful experiences, but you also have a ton of hardship that feels like life is burning you. This is all because you came to this life to deliberately develop the human conditioning you need for your greatest growth. Everyone's greatest growth comes through the difficult experiences in life because these experiences force us to grow. Think about this; if everything is going well, why change, right? So things need to not be going so well so that we are challenged in our beliefs, our ways of being and our internal thought processes so that we change. What you are doing here in this body, on this Earth is growing your soul's capacity to exist through balanced, wise, expansive love and that expansion comes through the burning of life.

Human conditioning—your internal beliefs about life, judgments for yourself and others, and internal emotions built by your experiences in life—is the key to your growth and is usually developed before the age of thirteen. Your human conditioning is specific to you and what you came to this big life classroom to learn. Before you came into your body you knew exactly what you were to learn. You basically understood; *Well, I need to learn this, and this, and this in this lifetime to grow my soul, so I will give myself that mother, that father, those siblings, and that partner. I will give myself this experience at this age and this one at another, and yes, that will give me enough dissatisfaction and wounding in life to do the job. Perfect!* You did this because you knew that you would develop the perfect human conditioning to bring the perfect hardship to yourself at the perfect times of your life. You set up your Calcination stage, or burning, perfectly.

You also knew that you would be learning and growing through the human ego.

The human ego has three purposes:
1. To perpetually keep you looking for love outside of yourself
2. To keep you desperately seeking acceptance and approval from others
3. To be seen as important and special through the eyes of others

Because of this perfectly designed, painful ego you will develop internal emotional drivers, both positive and negative. Those emotional drivers will then create reactionary behaviors, personal needs, triggers and internal chatter. All of these side effects of the unique emotional drivers you develop inside of yourself will bring about your perfect learning through believing you are being judged, hurt, wounded, a victim, betrayed, rejected, bullied, controlled, powerless or manipulated. None of these are bad, as you will see later in the stages of alchemy. However, I will validate that they sure feel bad as you are going through them. Learning lessons through these beliefs can be extremely painful. The best way to put it is that it just plain sucks!

This Calcination stage is the fire and brimstone whereby you are being burned by life. You are stuck in self-deceptions, illusions, fear, and internal pain caused by your ego-self. If you understand tarot cards, then you know that the Ego card is called The Devil. If you want to know what hell is like, well, you're in it and the only devil that exists is your own ego. This Earth is the Devil's lair where you are being burned by the false beliefs of the ego, and self-judgment is at an all-time high; unless, of course, you are completely immersed in the young soul stage where judgment of others is at an all-time high. The young soul stage is full of narcissists. I laugh as I remember a woman once telling me, "Oh, God loves narcissists! They help so many of us move through our lessons in life." I laugh because I have been burned by all too many narcissists. These young souls may not show up so nice in this life, but they sure do bring you the perfect wounding, betrayal or rejection needed to move you through your learning. I personally think it is more like being dropkicked than moved, but either way, you do learn.

Through this Calcination burning stage, we develop a heavy consciousness completely bullied by mind chatter. Our mind chatter has been called the disease of the mind for a reason. We are completely poisoned in our thinking by our conditioning and our ego-driven chatter brain becomes dominant. The chatter brain tends to keep us in linear, closed-minded and compartmentalized thinking that keeps us over-thinking, overanalyzing, over planning, taking things personally and projecting our insecurities and emotional triggers onto others.

Although it sounds bad to have a diseased chatter brain, it is perfect because in this stage of alchemy you need to build up enough human conditioning, or be burned enough in life, to motivate you to burn in a different way. When you hit a wall and you have experienced all of the human conditioning you can take, you will either hit rock bottom in your life, get completely depressed, fall into an apathetic state or you will realize that you absolutely cannot go on like you are and something in your life MUST change. At this point, congratulations, you have now completed your Calcination stage! You have successfully been reduced to a pile of ashes.

Have you ever heard the saying, *You are a phoenix, rising up out of the ash*? Well, in this Calcination stage you create your ashes so that you can rise up like the Phoenix. The Phoenix is a mythical bird of great beauty said to live for years in the desert to burn itself so that it can rise up out of the ashes in the freshness of youth. It then lives through another cycle of years, often an emblem of re-born idealism and hope. We are that Phoenix who came to Earth to experience rising up out of our pain and suffering, or human conditioning, into a more expanded, beautiful bird of wisdom. Once we do that, we will exist as a balanced, internally loving person who others will want to emulate.

Nicely done human conditioning, you have burned the Phoenix and the stage is now set for transformation. Once you have amassed all of the painful human conditioning, what you can also refer to as the textbooks needed for your specific soul lessons, you can now engage in a more deliberate calcination, or burning. This is where you deliberately burn through your false beliefs about yourself and this life, and consequently

53

surface the human conditioning created within you. For you to move to the next stage of alchemy, Dissolution, you must be able to see and acknowledge what has been built within you during the Calcination stage. What are your emotional drivers (see figure 5)? What needs have you developed (see figure 6)? What emotional triggers (see figure 7) have you developed that cause reactionary behaviors (see figure 8)? What internal chatter creates your story about you and life (see figure 9)? For you to heal what is broken within you it is necessary to expose it. It is like you are shining a mental flashlight inside of you so that the festering wounds of your human conditioning buried deep within can no longer remain in the dark.

Emotional Drivers

What positive **emotions** do you experience on a regular basis?

□ love for others	□ Love of self
□ Appreciation of others	□ Appreciation of self
□ Encouragement of others	□ Encouragement of self
□ Compassion for others	□ Compassion for self
□ Acceptance of others	□ Acceptance of self
□ Other	

What negative **emotions** do you experience on a regular basis?

□ Insecurity	□ Feeling like you are a bad person
□ Anger	□ Lack of emotion
□ Sadness	□ Guilt
□ Depression	□ Anxiety
□ Self-loathing	□ Feeling rejected
□ Worthlessness	□ Feeling hurt
□ Feeling superior	
□ Feeling like you are never good enough	
□ Other	

Figure 5

Personal Needs

What personal **needs** do you know are present in your life?

☐ To be right   ☐ To be important
☐ To have attention   ☐ To be center of attention
☐ To feel special   ☐ To be justified
☐ To be respected   ☐ To be better than other
☐ To feel power   ☐ To be validated
☐ To have control   ☐ To be heard
☐ To be seen   ☐ To be told you are loved
☐ To be supported   ☐ To be acknowledged
☐ Other _____

Figure 6

Personal Triggers

Which of these situations cause you to have an immediate negative reaction, whether internal or external?

☐ When someone criticizes me
☐ When an authority figure tells me what to do
☐ When someone tries to make me feel guilty
☐ When someone asks me what is wrong
☐ When someone says something about my weight or looks
☐ When someone looks at me wrong
☐ When someone is dismissive of me
☐ When someone needs to be right
☐ When someone can't take a suggestion
☐ When gives me a suggestion
☐ When someone needs to be the authority on everything
☐ When someone talks openly about sexual content
☐ When someone needs to be right
☐ When someone tries controlling me
☐ When someone needs to be the center of attention
☐ Other _____

Figure 7

Reactionary Behaviors

What reactionary **behaviors** tend to surface in your life?

☐ Disengagement   ☐ Abusive
☐ Selfishness   ☐ Demanding
☐ Gossiping   ☐ Critical of others
☐ Excessive crying   ☐ Disrespectful
☐ Dismissive of others   ☐ Rejection of others
☐ Yelling   ☐ Complaining
☐ Intolerance   ☐ Controlling others
☐ Controlling environment   ☐ Judging others
☐ Over indulgence (food, drugs, alcohol, exercise, preening, etc.)
☐ Other _____

Figure 8

Negative Mental Chatter

What kind of chatter goes on in either the background or foreground of your mind?

☐ I'm not good enough   ☐ I'm lazy
☐ I do not look good enough   ☐ I'm not a good person
☐ People think I'm weird   ☐ I'm invisible to others
☐ People are judging me   ☐ No one hears me
☐ I'm not smart enough   ☐ I can't
☐ I'm not successful enough   ☐ I have bad luck
☐ I'm unlovable   ☐ People don't like me
☐ I can't do anything right   ☐ People don't believe in me
☐ I over think, over plan and over analyze
☐ Other _____

Figure 9

Many people fear exposing the difficult parts of their lives because they are worried that if they open that Pandora's Box of buried memories and emotions they may not come back sane. They are afraid that they will fall down the rabbit hole of depression, misery or anger and lose mental or emotional control. Unfortunately, what happens if you keep your mental and emotional pain buried and do not expose it, is it continues to have control over you. You uncontrollably trigger when there is judgment of you, or you react with a negative behavior, either internally or externally, when an old emotion is momentarily exposed. By openly and purposefully exposing the truth of what is hidden inside of you, it no longer has control of you. To further explore your human conditioning, try creating a timeline of your life to reflect on what may be lurking beneath the surface (see figure 10).

Human Conditioning Timeline

On a piece of paper, write out age 0 to your current age. Next to each age, make notes about anything you remember that helped to build your human conditioning in this lifetime. Think about the of events, feelings, and life experiences that built your human conditioning.

Examples might be; bullying in grade school, a divorce, being ridiculed, deciding you were not attractive, losing a job, remembering feeling worthless, etc..

Reflecting on your timeline, what human conditioning did you build within yourself? Write what beliefs, judgments or feelings you have about the following:

Yourself:

Family:

Relationships (friends, intimate, teachers, etc.):

Society:

Your talents:

Career/school:

Money:

Safety/security:

Figure 10

During my Calcination stage I was really sick, physically. I had nine different medical issues— asthma, chronic sinusitis, fibromyalgia, spastic colon, Keinbocks Disease, hip defects, pain from a broken vertebrae, allergies, and food intolerances. I was constantly dealing with a cold, the flu or just feeling lousy. Mentally, I was full of negative internal chatter and struggled with feeling comfortable in social situations. I literally wanted to crawl under a rock every time I was out in public where I needed to interact with people.

My Calcination stage came to an end after leaving a very unhealthy relationship. I had hit my wall. I had hit rock bottom. I had been going from bad relationship to bad relationship. I was making good money but couldn't manage it to save my life. I was constantly in pain, constantly sick, had just finished my eleventh operation, and my life was full of negative drama. I woke up one morning realizing I could not go on like that anymore. In complete desperation, I called my friend Renee, an intuitive holistic healer, and through a face full of snot and tears I blurted out to her that I could not do this anymore. I could not be sick, I could not have another bad relationship, I could not be broke and I could not have another operation. I had had it! I remember that Renee actually breathed a sigh of relief when I told her this and said, "Oh, you're finally ready." I also remember that I was immediately catapulted into my ego-self and angrily yelled, "What! What do you mean ready? I could have done something about this earlier? Why didn't you help me?" She was so patient. She said, "Kelly, describe yourself to me." and I immediately went into my on-the-surface personality and started describing how I thought other people saw me. "Well." I said with false confidence, "I am confident, energetic, smart, loving, a good mom..." She stopped me there. In a bit of an exhausted tone she said, "Ok, let's go behind all that." My first instincts inside were to think *Oh shit* and fear hit as I realized she wanted me to get vulnerable. I was not quite willing to go there so she said something about me that I do not remember, but I do know that it sent me into a tailspin. I began telling her that what she said was mean and I could not believe she had said it about me. She was again so patient, but firm, and again forced the issue of me looking deep inside of myself and seeing what I thought of myself. After I realized I was not going to get out of speaking my truth, I broke down. I began sobbing in defeat as I realized what I saw deep inside of me. I saw four statements about myself, and they were not pretty. I saw that I thought I was a bad person, I was a worthless person, I was a sick person and I was a broken person. I knew it to be true. Once I dropped the façade' of who I was in other people's eyes and looked inside of myself I saw what was driving my triggers, behaviors and needs—I did not like who I was.

For me to complete my Calcination stage, I needed to open up into my vulnerability. That was the only way I was going to expose old wounds and harsh self-beliefs. I had to acknowledge what was lurking there beneath the surface of what I wanted to believe about myself, but truly didn't. I had to be honest with myself about the feelings I carried inside of me. Although it was painful to see it, that moment changed my life.

Yes, we are burned by life, and yes, we chose this. We chose to become the Phoenix and burn ourselves so that we can rise up bigger, stronger and wiser. Once we are burned, we then need to look at the ash that is left. By not fearing what we will see, we then expose what we want to dissolve from our inner being, hence, enter the second stage of alchemy, the Dissolution stage.

Summary of the Calcination Stage

- This is the stage where you develop your human experiences
- Your human experiences, upbringing, influential people in your life, personal characteristics and genetics shape you
- You have an ego that causes you to fear being rejected, betrayed or unloved because it keeps you looking for love, acceptance and importance outside of yourself
- You develop human conditioning in order to believe you are not enough
- All of this is the burning of life, or Calcination you need to learn life lessons that will allow you to grow and expand into unconditional love
- This is the alchemical stage of setting you up to break you down

Chapter Two
Dissolution
To undo or break down

Soul's work is hard work, but it's the only work that makes your life easy

---

Reminder of the Alchemical Stages

Stage 1: Calcination:
To convert with heat or burning (human conditioning)

Stage 2: Dissolution:
To undo or break down (heal internal wounding)

Stage 3: Separation:
Breaking apart or letting go (see the ego when it shows up)

Stage 4: Conjunction:
Union (balance your opposites)

Stage 5: Fermentation:
Change (Dark night of your soul and golden light)

Stage 6: Distillation:
Purification (let go of old habits and safety zones)

Stage 7: Coagulation:
To change into a thicker, stronger mass

Stage two in learning to alchemize your soul is called Dissolution. It is not the most difficult stage to reach, but it is certainly the most involved process to move through. People will either spend much of their lives in step one, Calcination—building and experiencing their human conditioning, or in step two, Dissolution—breaking down the ego control, moving into self-forgiveness, and letting go of old beliefs and patterns that keep them stuck in pain, self-judgment and lack of self worth.

When an alchemist is working with plant, mineral or animal matter in the Dissolution stage they will use water or acid to break down the ash created in the Calcination stage. They are dissolving the ash to set it up for the next stage in alchemy, which is the Separation stage. This seems like a pretty simple stage, right? Just throw a little water or acid in, mix it up and voila; you are done with stage two. It might be simple with a metal or organic matter, but dissolving your human "ash", well that is another story.

Dissolution of the soul is called a return to innocence, or a time of rebirth. No, I am not necessarily talking about the Born Again Christian kind of rebirth; I am talking about rebirthing a new you mentally and emotionally. During this phase you examine the beliefs, patterns and emotions, also known as the human conditioning, that you developed in your Calcination stage, and learn to dissolve those beliefs that are false. This is the stage where you release negative emotions, heal old memories, heal your younger selves, who I call your younger "yous," and create new patterns of living a more self-loving life.

During this time, you expose the ego and repressed thoughts and feelings continuously so as to release, or dissolve, the false personality; also known as the human-conditioned personality. You dissolve the false personality to set yourself up for the next stage of healing, the Separation stage. In the Separation stage the authentic you, or genuine you, begins to emerge. In order for you to find, acknowledge and adopt the authentic traits of yourself without your human conditioning taking over you first must learn about self-love, self-forgiveness and develop within you a feeling that you are worth expanding into the divinely beautiful being that you are. This requires that you break down those parts that are not healthy, or self-loving.

Letting go of pain, resentment, anger, betrayal, abandonment, and rejection is not easy. I have heard others in the spiritual healing world often say, "It's easy! All you have to do is just let it go!" When I hear that I want to start breaking out into Disney's "Frozen" theme song and dance around dreamily in a glittery gown because that is how fairytale I would feel if I told one of my client's to just *let it go!* Our human conditioning takes a firm hold of us and creates beliefs within us that are drilled deep into our psyche and tissue. It is not just going to break apart because we think it to be so. Oh, sure, in our wise-woman or wise-man state, also called our matured state, we can get into a mindset of forgiving our parents, forgiving a perpetrator, or understanding why a bad situation happened to us, but that alone does not typically change the internal programming you have built deep inside of you. This is why, even if you mentally forgive someone or something that happened, you still have a negative charge, negative emotion or emotional trigger around it.

I remember back, before my time of Dissolution, I was doing a, "Claiming Your Power Back" meditation. In this meditative state, we ask people in our lives to give us back a stone that represents the power they either took from us or we gave away to them. In this meditation I claimed back a beautiful purple stone from my ex-boyfriend, a green one from my ex-husband, a shimmering golden one from my mother, and a whole series of other awe inspiring stones from others in my life. At the end of the meditation, my dad's spirit came forward and slapped a massive, gray lump of misshapen rock in my hand. In my mind I remember just staring at it, not looking up at my dad and not being able to have any response at all. Thank goodness the person leading the meditation asked us to come back at that time, relieving me of my internal immobility. I came out of that meditation completely stunned. I had no idea why my dad gave me that lump of gray shit and everyone else gave me beautiful stones. In my wise-woman state I had no anger for my dad; I forgave him, understood him and had a great relationship with him, I saw him as a beautiful person. Consciously I felt that way, but sub-consciously there was something lurking that I needed to heal with him. It was not until I had entered into my Dissolution stage, and began dredging up what needed to be healed within me, that I found I had a massive amount of anger and resentment toward my dad. Those emotions of my human conditioning needed to be worked through mentally and emotionally so that spiritually I could move into a more healed, self-loving and father-loving me. Even though I was in a loving, forgiving state with him at that time, that did not mean that I was not carrying old emotions and pain inside of me that would inevitably, and had indeed, shown up as emotional triggers. That gray rock in my meditation was my subconscious mind telling me I had something to deal with, even though my present conscious mind felt love and forgiveness.

To be clear, my father is a good man and my anger and resentment had more to do with my fiery personality and personal decision to bury my clairvoyance from the world than it had to do with him. I was just projecting it onto him because I was hurt within my own being. By exposing my pain around him, I only exposed the pain I had created within myself.

64

In the Dissolution stage, it is essential for you to move deeper into your vulnerability to see what is lurking inside, underneath the conscious state of your current thoughts. What is the background noise you are hearing internally, what are those repressed feelings triggering inside of you, and what are the hidden beliefs you have developed about yourself or others saying? Accessing these hidden, repressed or festering internal wounds from our human conditioning are the key to moving through the Dissolution stage. Our subconscious beliefs are what are governing our internal needs and external reactions, also known as emotional triggers.

So why do you need to access these? Biologically, what has occurred in your body is that your neurons—nerve cells that provide the pathways to create learning and beliefs, or thoughts—have created belief patterns within you that came from your human conditioning. Beliefs such as, *I'm not good enough, people think I'm weird,* or *I never have enough money.* These patterns will continue running inside of you until you heal enough internally to break your neural pathways apart and create new pathways. On top of that, you also have a charge around memories; a positive one around happy memories, a neutral charge around inconsequential memories and a negative one around not so happy memories. You cannot solely think away these charges and internal beliefs in your head, or brain, because your head-brain is only part of the solution.

You have three brains—the head-brain, the heart-brain and the gut-brain—and all three are connected together. Yes, you have neurons, which allow you to think and learn, in your heart as well as in your gut. To see the research on this visit Heartmath.org and you will find a plethora of information about these three brains and how they work together as one big network of beliefs, emotions and energetic charges. Since these three brains work together, this means that if there is a brain in your head and your heart, your self-love must be in alignment with your thoughts, and if there is a brain in your gut then that means that your internal emotions must be in alignment with both your self-love and your thoughts, which is why you cannot simply "think" away your human conditioning.

That might seem a little complex to apply to yourself. But having applied this process of letting go of old wounds and negative emotional drivers in thousands of session with people, and personally experiencing it myself, I can tell you it is a pretty straightforward, logical process. Here it is:

1. Gain an understanding in your **head-brain** about what this life is: why you are here, why you developed the human conditioning you did, what the people in your life were teaching you, and why you should forgive yourself and others (Chapter one);

2. Allow yourself to go through an internal healing process where you feel love and compassion for the younger "yous" (ages of you prior to today) in your **heart-brain**. This is necessary because these younger selves are the ones who experienced and built your human conditioning. Nurture them, feel compassion for them and forgive them for they are an integral part of your growth experience here on earth. Learn to

66

love those younger selves and accept them as a necessary part of your experience, even if it was a painful, shameful or hurtful experience they went through. Thank them for taking on the part of your journey where you developed the human conditioning you needed to learn your soul lessons here on Earth. If it weren't for their painful experiences you could not expand your soul and move into a deeper, more unconditionally loving person;

3. Feel inside your **gut-brain** for the emotions you are ready to release and heal, and let go of negative emotional charges associated with those younger selves. Work with these younger selves to let go of old beliefs about yourself that are not true. See the beauty in them and in you.

This is it: the three-step process of the Dissolution stage, also considered a holistic healing approach. Holistic means whole and that means that you address the mental you, the emotional you and the spiritual you together. In other words, you address the head-brain, the heart-brain and the gut-brain together. In this stage you also address the physical you, but I am saving that for its own book since your physical state is a direct result of your mental, emotional and spiritual states of being.

Remember how I had found my four statements about myself when I hit my rock bottom in my Calcination stage; the *I am a bad, worthless, sick and broken person* statements? Well, finding those statements was just the beginning of my healing. Later that afternoon, after learning of these brutal statements I had buried so effectively in my subconscious mind, I got deep into meditation. In this meditation I asked to be shown "why?" I needed to know why I believed that I was bad and worthless? I somewhat understood sick and broken, but bad? Worthless? Those were some pretty harsh beliefs to have about myself.

I must have had a lot of help from above on that day, because not having a lot of experience at that time with meditation; I sunk immediately, deeply in. That meditation was intense; emotion and memory flew at me so quickly that it felt like I was in that meditation for five minutes, but the amount of what I was shown and the emotions I released could never have been revealed in that short of time. For an hour and a half I was shown memory after memory—being bullied on the playground, being called "Dog Face Kelly", feeling forgotten and unimportant, rejection from friends, my fighting with my parents and sisters, my divorce, inappropriate sexual experiences in high school, desperately wanting more nurturing as a child, partying as a teen, hating myself, getting fired as an adult, and the list goes on. I brought my younger selves in to my meditation and told them I understood why they were the way they were and why they did what they did. I loved them, forgave them and cried with them. I held their hands, hugged them and let them release insecurities, pain from memories, guilt, shame, fear, and regret. It was the most lovingly painful experience I had ever had. At the end of the meditation I was also shown two past lives that were still affecting me in this lifetime, which I would later use to understand more about myself, and how my conditioning was developed so deeply in this lifetime. In this meditation I broke apart the conditioned beliefs held within my head, heart and gut neurons, that told me I was bad and worthless. I saw that I was beautiful and worthy. I saw that I loved me, even when I was not being nice, not respecting myself or others, or feeling guilt, shame or self-loathing. I saw that I was a product of my human experience and that I did not have to hold that human conditioning in my being. I was a good person and a worthy person and that meditation helped me to let go, or dissolve, my unwanted beliefs about myself that were not true.

Throughout the next year I continued to look inside of myself, healing my younger "mes" and exposing painful internal truths about myself. I found so many ugly parts that I had to expose so that they could no longer hold me prisoner. I found that I was addicted to drama with other people because it kept me from looking at my own drama inside of myself. I saw that I was addicted to being a victim and used my illnesses and injuries to keep myself in a victim status. I found I loved the attention being a victim gave me because I desperately needed love and acceptance. I found that I created illness and injuries in my body not only for the attention, but because it was a subconscious form of self-punishment due to my not liking who I was. Amongst all of those truths, I also found that I liked the authentic me, believed I was a good person, and liked the wise me I was becoming.

Throughout this year of healing, I was shown a couple of key understandings that really helped me heal. One was what I refer to as the Four Facts of self-forgiveness. Understanding these four facts allowed me to move into self-forgiveness and I now give this understanding to my clients as I work them through healing and forgiving themselves.

The fact is that humans are always looking for four things in our lives:

1. To be loved and accepted for who we are and what we do;
2. To be seen and heard by others in a healthy way;
3. To be nurtured when we are young and have loving touch when we are older;
4. To feel supported.

I call these the Four Facts of Forgiveness because if at any time in our lives we are not getting them, we are desperately looking for them, or we never got them as a child, we have misguided actions as a result. In other words, we often engage in things like betray ourselves or others, make decisions that take us in a difficult direction in our lives, react in ways that are harmful to ourselves or others, or engage in acts that we later regret if we did not get these four things.

These four facts of internal desire are beautiful things to want, it is just that when they are not present in our lives the way we want them or they are continuously sought outside of ourselves, they cause us to act in desperation and need, which does not make for a positive foundation to live from. Understanding that your actions, although perhaps misguided or self-depreciating, are in search of these four loving things allows you to move closer to a place of understanding and forgiveness of self.

When we chose to enter this life, we purposefully give ourselves an ego, which we now know is a person's sense of self-esteem and self-importance. This ego keeps us perpetually looking for love, acceptance and self-importance outside of ourselves through the Four Facts of Forgiveness.

When we cannot find love, acceptance and self-importance through other people, we feel a lack of self-worth, which causes irrational, self-depreciating thought and behavior. This may sound bad, but this is actually quite perfect because this desire to find your worth outside of yourself actually catapulted you right into your human conditioning. You purposefully came here to develop this conditioning because it brings you down so you know what to pick up. It takes away from you what you need to learn to claim, such as self-love, empowerment, compassion, ease of being, forgiveness, gentleness, humility, moderation or acceptance. There is purpose to the perceived madness of the ego.

Another view of life that helped me move through my own forgiveness was when my Guides shared with me that I should consider my life to be like a big geometric puzzle. They explained that each piece of our life puzzle fits perfectly together and each puzzle piece represents a piece of how each individual's human conditioning was built (see figure 12). They said that the puzzle pieces are made up of memories, people in your life who influenced you, your upbringing, your genetics, your astrological sign, your experiences in life, and so on. At any given time, when you are about to make a decision in your life or react or behave in a certain way, the only puzzle piece that fits next is a result of where you are at in your mental and emotional state at that given time. No other puzzle piece could fit unless you had different experiences, different influences or different people in your life that built a different human conditioned piece. Therefore, it doesn't pay to judge yourself harshly for a mistake you made. Take time to look at the *why* of what you did what you did. Understand how you got to that place and what human conditioning led you there. It is through that understanding of the *why* that healing and self-forgiveness can take place.

I often have clients who beat themselves up mercilessly for doing something they think is absolutely unforgiveable. A very difficult experience I work people through is the aftermath of having an abortion. They tell me that they should never be forgiven because they killed an innocent child and did wrong. I am absolutely not going to make a statement about the rightness or wrongness around this topic but am using this experience because it is heavily charged and one that many believe is unforgiveable.

Let's imagine, for the sake of explanation, that we have a woman who was born into a society or a family where being an unmarried woman having a child was unacceptable. When speaking to her I would ask her to reflect on where she was at mentally and emotionally in her life at that time. What were the conditions she was living in; were they emotionally supportive, physically healthy? Were they mentally unstressed? I'd ask her about her self-esteem at that time; did she like herself, respect herself and where was her sense of self-worth? I'd ask her to think about where she was at with all of these when she decided to have sex. I'd ask what her beliefs were about premarital sex, what was the motivation behind her engaging, what was she looking for emotionally? I'd explain that those feelings and beliefs were built by her personal geometric puzzle. At the time she had premarital sex, and at the time she decided to have an abortion, she had one puzzle piece that fit each time due to the mental and emotional state she was in at that moment. This does not make her a bad soul, an evil person, or a shameful person. She is nothing more than a product of her current

72

human conditioning developed by the life she lived, the upbringing she had, her personality traits, her genetics, and the age of her soul. This could also be a part of her life contract, to have that experience here in this lifetime. That experience is part of the human conditioning she came to engage in, whether considered right or wrong to our society. To source, there is no concrete understanding of right or wrong, just experiences that lead you to live a life of internal and external beauty. The "wrong" experiences are teachers to move us into a place within ourselves that is lived from unconditional love and compassion.

It is important to understand that our souls are moving toward balance, self-love and self-acceptance within ourselves. It is in this state of being that we will not feel the need to engage in harmful, detrimental, judgmental, intolerant or violent behaviors inside of or outside of ourselves. I completely understand *Thou shalt not kill* and *Do unto others as you would have done to you* beliefs. We hold an ideal of doing good and being good in this world because that is an innate understanding of the innate beauty we hold within our soul. However, it is important to understand that we are immersed in conditioning here. We are full of expectations, judgment, comparisons, feelings of rejection and unworthiness. This makes it very difficult to engage in authentic unconditional love. If you judge someone for doing wrong or being bad, that is not unconditional in its love. Ask yourself, how can you be authentically unconditional in your love if you are immersed in all of this conditioning? It is equally important to understand that we did not come here wise, flawless or perfect in our goodness. We are here learning about that and how to find it within, through the needs and behaviors of the ego. Our mistakes are our teachers and to be balanced in our unconditional love we must value them as much as we value the times we do good.

I'd explain this to my client who had her abortion. Then I'd point out the Four Factors of Forgiveness. I'd ask her what would have happened if she'd had that child? Would she be seen in a healthy way by others? Would her family have supported her? Would she fear she would never have loving relationship again in her life? Would she feel society would accept her? I'd point out that her decision was due to fear of losing love, acceptance, being seen well, and support. And this is all compounded by the fear of not having an emotional and physically loving relationship in the future due to the potential stain upon her character. This is a normal human response to life. I'd ask, "Are you going to judge yourself for, well, being human?"

This stage of dissolving is all about forgiveness and dissolving false beliefs about our self and others. To enter into forgiveness it is important to understand all of the *whys* of forgiveness.

Why did you develop your sense of self-worth, or lack of self-worth?
Why did you develop your personal needs?
Why did you develop your personal emotional triggers or reactionary behaviors?
Why do you have the parents you do?
Why did you have the experiences in life you have had?

Remember, this life is a classroom and you chose your parents and early experiences so that you could develop the perfect human conditioning you needed for your lessons. As you move through life you will either learn lessons—your personal karma—from your human conditioning or not. As you learn your lessons you will move forward into a more peaceable, healthy life; and if you do not, you will continuously draw to you the experiences, people and situations you need until the lesson is learned. To learn a lesson, you need to make enough mistakes around the subject so that you can gain the wisdom needed to not make them again. You need to project onto others enough, fail enough, beat yourself up enough, judge others enough, etc. so that you can clearly see what does not work, so that you can move with wisdom into what does.

Your reaction is your lesson.
How you react to that lesson is your learning.

I say this so often to clients. What I am trying to point out is that this stage of Dissolution is all about internal learning and finding internal love. It is realizing that you will react in not so nice ways in this life, guaranteed, and you need to know that this is what you came here for. If you are continuously beating yourself up for every time you make a mistake, or act in a not so nice way, you will never move into a place of appreciating the very lessons you came here to learn. You need to love your mistakes because they are your greatest teachers. If you have a reaction in life you did not like, understand why the reaction was there. Instead of beating yourself up for your mistakes, try looking inside and understand what was triggered, why you are hurting or what caused your reaction. Watch how you react to yourself internally when you have a bad reaction externally; it is then that you will engage in your learning, consequently having a better reaction externally.

The Dissolution stage is a time to realize that it is not necessary to find love, acceptance and self-worth outside of yourself, because you just ARE love. How can you ever seek to gain love outside of yourself when it was always a part of you to begin with?

In this stage you find love through self-forgiveness and self-acceptance. In this stage:

1. Take time to focus on your healing
2. Acknowledge your personal triggers, needs and reactionary behaviors
3. Understand that this life is a classroom where you are experiencing all that life has to offer, whether it is good, bad, ugly or beautiful
4. Allow yourself to go through a process of forgiving yourself and others because you understand that we are all on a unique journey of human conditioning
5. Realize that it is the ego that keeps us looking for self-importance through the eyes of others and all that does is keep us away from seeing how beautiful we are internally
6. Take the time to heal your younger "yous" so that you can accept every age of you as a beautiful part of your experience, whether it was a hard age or not
7. Understand that each age of soul is perfect and necessary and find tolerance and compassion for anyone at any stage, including yourself
8. Begin to realize that if you ARE love and radiate love, then you cannot really be betrayed or rejected because that can only

happen if you are looking for love and acceptance outside of yourself

9. Begin to realize that you cannot be a victim if you are the one who is drawing to you the people necessary to reflect to you what you still have that is broken within you (explained further in the Separation stage)

Allow yourself to be in this stage as long as it takes to heal your younger selves and forgive yourself and others for having human conditioning. Allow yourself to return to innocence by breaking down what is broken within you and building, or rebirthing, a more beautiful you who operates from a place of self-love. Expose your repressed pain, false beliefs, fears and false personality so that you can now move forward in freeing yourself from the ego in the Separation stage of the alchemical process.

Summary of the Dissolution Stage

- This is the stage where you dissolve the false beliefs you created about yourself and others in the Calcination stage
- This is a time of acknowledging the pain, emotional drivers, internal wounding, and false beliefs that are a result of your personal human conditioning
- Bring yourself though a process of healing your younger "yous"; loving them and accepting them as a perfect part of your growth in this lifetime
- Forgive yourself and others for having conditioning, the ego and being human
- Keep internally focused, letting other people's issues remain theirs, while you seek to find self love

---

Chapter Three
Separation
Breaking apart or letting go

Until you learn to see the perfection in the lessons of the ego, it will keep you in a perpetual headlock of pain and disillusionment

---

Reminder of the Alchemical Stages

Stage 1: Calcination:
To convert with heat or burning (human conditioning)

Stage 2: Dissolution:
To undo or break down (heal internal wounding)

Stage 3: Separation:
Breaking apart or letting go (see the ego when it shows up)

Stage 4: Conjunction:
Union (balance your opposites)

Stage 5: Fermentation:
Change (Dark night of your soul and golden light)

Stage 6: Distillation:
Purification (let go of old habits and safety zones)

Stage 7: Coagulation:
To change into a thicker, stronger mass

In the process of alchemizing plant, animal or metal, alchemists use the Separation stage to isolate the desired components from the undesired components that were developed in the Calcination stage and broken down in the Dissolution stage. They do this by filtering, cutting, settling or agitating with air. After doing this, the unworthy material is discarded and they are left with the material they consider worthy of the remaining alchemical processes. They are left with a good foundation from which to build something new.

After my year of dissolving what I thought was bad, worthless, sick and broken about myself I remember feeling so good. I had done so much healing and had learned to find that I wasn't a bad or worthless person at all. I genuinely liked who I was for the first time that I could remember. I had forgiven so many previous "mes" and let them release the painful emotion they had carried for so long. At this point in my healing I actually remember thinking *I am healed!* Little did I know that my journey of healing was not done, it was going to get even better.

Consider the alchemical healing process like peeling away layers of an onion; once you peel one layer you reveal another layer and you keep on peeling until you get to the core. Imagine you develop the layers of the onion in your Calcination stage and then begin pealing them in the Dissolution stage. Think about an onion's layers; the outer layers are harder, weaker, thinner, are not pleasant to eat and are discarded, where the inner layers are thicker and juicier and palatable. I equate that to my outer emotional layers let go in the Dissolution stage. I let go of hardened, weak, shallow, unpleasant parts of me to reveal a deeper, juicier me who I found so much more palatable to myself and others. After the second stage of Dissolution, I had moved into a basic level of self-love and although my ego was still present, it was no longer burning me with my human conditioning. I began to understand the purpose of this life and the perfection of the internal wounding that was developed as a result. Because I moved through that wounding, I now had a good foundation within myself from which to build something new; a stronger, deeper, wiser me.

In the Separation stage, we are separating ourselves from the ego. Well, we don't completely remove ourselves from it because, after all, we are human and will continue to have an ego, it's just that after this stage of Separation we will not be ruled by the ego. We separate ourselves so that we can look at the ego when it shows up from an outside perspective. We notice when it wants to keep us in a place of need, like the need to be right, validated, in control, special, better than, and so on. We also recognize our reactionary behaviors and triggers, which happen less and less as we learn self-love, as aspects of the ego that are still looking for love and acceptance outside of ourselves.

In this stage we see the ego from a birds-eye view and call it out when it shows up. I remember the first time I totally saw I needed to be right all of the time. I was shocked, not that I was shocked that I wanted to be right, but that I didn't see it before then. I remember asking myself *How could you not have seen this before?* Realizing how embarrassed I was, that others must have recognized that in me too. It is so funny, until we are ready to see our ego-based needs and behaviors, we are completely blind to them. I suppose this is good because as I said earlier, until we make enough mistakes around a life subject, we don't learn and gain wisdom around it. We need to stay blinded to the ego and in our human conditioning long enough to gain experience through our mistakes as well as our successes. When we amass enough of these good, bad, beautiful and ugly reactions to a life lesson. we can then learn the lesson and move through into something better.

One of my massive life lessons was to realize I was not a victim, and much of that lesson was centered around manipulative people, particularly women. Throughout my life, I had brought in person after person who I believed hurt me, treated me badly, or betrayed me. Each time they presented themselves in my life, I had a big story to tell around whatever had transpired. A story all about how much of an awful person they were and how I was completely victimized by their bad behavior. I would tell anyone who would listen, and looked to my "audience" to validate my story of victimhood. I always had a list of proof about how bad they were, absolutely sure that any court of law would have supported my claim that they were indeed big bad baddies who deserved to be shunned by society and never befriended again.

At that time I had no clue that I was the one who drew these people to me and I equally had no idea that I was the one bringing out this behavior in them because I had yet to learn that I was not a victim. I was oblivious to the fact that what I thought, felt and believed, consciously and subconsciously, was actually signaling to the world whether I had learned this lesson or not. I had no idea that I was in control of the people and situations that came into my life, and also that it was absolutely perfect. It is crucial that this concept of *you drew this person or situation to you in order to learn your lessons* is fully understood. If it is not, you will continue to feel a victim to life, or others, and will not be able to move through this stage of Separation.

In 2011, my Guides began teaching me about sacred geometry and how the world is made of nothing but mathematical equations. In my mind's eye they would take me into a room of geometry and highlight particular shapes, giving me an instantaneous understanding of what mathematical concept they wanted me to understand. I couldn't even begin to recap or even recall the information that they shared, it was just there and I would ethereally hear them say, "Do you understand?" and without consciously knowing what I understood, I knew I did indeed understand what they were explaining to me. It was as though I understood at a cellular and soul level, but not at a head level. After each highlighted shape was presented, I had a greater understanding of how the universe ran and what this life was about. It transformed me greatly. Without knowing why I knew what I knew, I understood the meaning of this life, it's purpose and how to teach people to navigate it.

What I have learned is that each leaf, our bodies, our waters, the air, situations, planets, reactions, illnesses, everything we perceive, is all a mathematical code. They explained that all of existence is like a big computer that is running based on the mathematical coding of source energy, individual peoples' actions and reactions, and the alignment of the planets combined. There isn't one set of mathematical principles that runs a computer, one for your body, one for source, and yet another one for the universe. All of existence is governed by the same mathematical principles. They also explained that we are inseparable from everything in existence and we are all affecting each other.

Let me explain this a little further. Our heartbeats are not steady; they have a high variation in the time interval between heartbeats. What my Guides have explained is that your heartbeat actually reflects your conscious and subconscious thoughts, feelings and beliefs; and as it beats, it is creating code for the universe to interpret. This is how manifesting works. You can find some wonderful research about heart rate variability done by the HeartMath Institute; however, you will not find research done around the code that is created for the universe to bring you your lessons. This is an explanation my Guides gave to me and you will have to listen to your internal truth meter for a determination as to whether or not it resonates with you. Either way, whether you understand that your heartbeat is coding that brings you your lessons or not, please understand that you are drawing to you what you need for your highest and greatest good.

What my Guides further explained is that this heartbeat code that is a mathematical code of how you think, feel and believe is sent into the world, the universe and all of existence though what they have shown in my mind's eye to be a grid. They have shown me this grid many times. I have seen it connecting us to each other, us to nature, us to the earth, and also connecting the suns and planets to each other. I usually see it with a green glow or green vibrating energy and it is vast. Below is an explanation of the grid that was taken from an interview with Gregg Braden titled, *Oneness and the Quantum Hologram*.

Almost universally, ancient texts and traditions say to us, in the language of their time, that we are part of all that we see, that we are related through a Force to the events of our world, to one another, to the processes within our bodies and the Cosmos and beyond. In our most sacred traditions, this Force is described as all-powerful, something that permeates all of Creation. It's not "out there" somewhere. It is a part of ourselves as well as a part of all that we perceive.

Now Western science, beginning in about 1993, through accredited academic and scientific institutions, has performed experiments with unexpected — and in some cases very surprising — results, experiments demonstrating that the ancient tenets appear to be true. In these experiments, the only way that the curious and bizarre behavior of nature and particles in the subatomic world, the quantum world, could be explained was if those particles were all connected through a previously unrecognized Force. So what's happening right now, in the early years of the 21st Century, is that Western science is moving toward accepting the ancient idea of this unity field that links all of Creation.

Some scientists are calling this

field Nature's Mind. Some scientists are calling it the Mind of God (a famous name given to it by Stephen Hawking in his book *A Brief History of Time.*) Many researchers now are calling it the Quantum Hologram

This unity field, this Quantum Hologram, responds to the things that we do and the way we think and feel. It allows us as individuals to participate in the events of our lives rather than feeling hopeless as we stand by and watch the world teeter on the brink of war, or watch our loved ones succumb to illness and diseases that we really don't understand.

Western scientists now not only identify this field, but they give it characteristics. They say that this field appears to be everywhere, all the time, a form of energy that's already present rather than being generated in one place and transmitted somewhere else.

It's everywhere all the time and appears to have been with us since Creation began, what physicists called the "Big Bang."

So it's always been here, it's everywhere all the time, and it

also appears to have what
Western scientists are now
calling "intelligence." It appears
to be an intelligent field in that
it responds to the language of
coherent human emotion.
Except for the language, this
field sounds very similar to
what the ancients called God.

I love this explanation of what I know as the grid.
Our heart's mathematical code is going into this
grid all the time and responding accordingly. We
are pre-coded with karma, what we are to learn
here in this lifetime. Before you came into a body,
you knew what you were to learn here so that you
could become wiser and more expanded as a soul.
These lessons allow you to expand your capacity
for unconditional love by experiencing the human
conditioning you need to work through for your
specific soul growth requirements. Ok, you know
this, so now imagine that you are living in a big
computer (the world) and you are a program that
is running in the computer. Your heartbeat is
creating new computer code with each shift in
thought, feeling and belief you have that are based
on the actions and reactions you have within this
world computer. Your personal heart-code is
programming the computer for a response, and of
course the computer can do nothing but supply
that response. The computer is constantly
adjusting all things within it based on each
individual's heart-code. Based on that heart beat
code your life constantly brings you situations,
people and circumstances to keep you learning the
life lessons you chose before you came into a body.
The computer doesn't think, analyze or punish; it
is just an automatic response to what you are
putting out.

This computer is not only complying with the heart-code *you* put into it, but it is complying with the heart-code of everyone. My Guides have shown me how every action we take has far reaching consequences.

Our actions, learning or lack of learning affects everything in existence. This is not said to cause you to feel overwhelmed, or produce guilt if you don't learn a lesson or have a not-so-nice reaction. It is said to explain that all things are connected and we are constantly affecting each other. Source has no judgment about how fast or slow you learn a lesson. Source has a universal understanding that you came here to make mistakes and muck things up royally so that you can learn and grow your soul. And remember, the world computer doesn't think or judge, it just responds.

A few years ago I was working with a client and we were communicating with his deceased mother's soul. He was asking me if she had orchestrated bringing his current girlfriend to him, because that would be so like her. She ethereally laughed and said to me in my mind's eye, "Oh, no, we don't do that!" and I was suddenly gone from the room. In my mind's eye I was seeing a vast universe of little points of light. There were billions of them and together they were emitting what looked like a blue mist around them; it was breathtaking. The thing that struck me was how this "blue mist" was moving in perfect synchronicity. As one point of light moved they all adjusted. It looked like how a blue silk fabric might look if you shook it in the air in slow motion. My client's soul-mother explained to me that each point of light is our soul here on earth, and we are constantly adjusting based on each other's actions and reactions. The points of light in the blue mist moved in response to each other in perfect synchronicity. I remembered how about a year earlier my Guides had tried to show me how much our actions affected a greater thing, but at the time I didn't get it. I did after seeing and understanding that magnificent blue mist—our actions don't just affect what we get back from the big world computer; it also affects everyone on the planet because we are all in a synchronistic experience together. What this says is that when you draw in someone to teach you something or give you an experience in something, they equally drew you in for their lesson or experience as well. Even when the experience is hard, you are not a victim to anyone or anything; you drew them in perfectly.

Bringing this explanation back to our heart-code, we are orchestrating situations, people, accidents, successes, malfunctions, and the miracles that happen in our lives. We draw to us what we need to satisfy the encoded lessons we have within us when we enter this life. When you learn and grow, you bring in a more positive happy life and when you don't, that's ok. Situations and types of people who show up in your life will just be repeated and repeated until you are ready to learn your lessons and move into a healthier, wiser you. Remember, when you amass enough mistakes and successes around a life lesson, you will learn it and move on in life in a better, more unconditionally loving way.

In this stage of Separation, it is important to understand that you are not a victim of life, you are creating it. You are writing the code for your life at every moment, and every moment is an opportunity for growth.

As you move through this stage of Separation from the ego, with the understanding that you are creating all of your life experiences, start to see how the ego has its own programming. The ego has programming to keep you perpetually looking for love and acceptance outside of yourself and for self-importance and worth through the eyes of others. Once you can see that ego programming, you can begin to override its power over you. In order to change the programming of the ego, and separate from it, you first have to see it at work.

During this phase of Separation, it is necessary to become internally narcissistic. I do not mean become the external narcissist who is continuously gratifying oneself through vain admiration of themselves based on how others see them. I mean to become an internal narcissist; someone who is constantly internally aware, obsessed in a way, with what is going on inside of you. It is important to constantly notice what is happening inside of you so that you can recognize the ego programming when it presents itself. During this stage, become the observer. Observe how you think and react internally and externally.

Are you acting out of need (see Figure 6, Chapter One)?
Are you projecting your own hurt, pain and internal wounding onto others (see Figure 8, Chapter One)?
Are you placing yourself into a victim mode?
Are you judging others?
Are you looking to others for love and acceptance?
Are you trying to be important to others?
Are you trying to be better than others?

Becoming the necessary narcissist means that you are taking time to see you and your behavior, not that of those around you. This is a time of understanding that **everyone and everything that shows up in your life is a mirror for you.** A mirror of what is working, not working, beautiful and broken inside of you. They are reflecting to you so that you see your own triggers, your own judgments, your own needs and your own internal wounding, and you are reflecting back to the world computer whether you understand or whether you need more experiences with your lessons. All of these lessons we are learning are bringing us to the understanding that we are love and cannot get it from outside of ourselves. You can understand that conceptually and can reiterate it all you want, but you cannot fool the world computer. How you think and feel about that at a subconscious and conscious level is tattling on you constantly.

When I was drawing manipulative people into my life, and time and again entering into my victim and judgment mode, those situations and people were reflecting to me that I still believed I could be hurt and the only way I could believe I could be hurt by another is if I was looking for love and acceptance outside of myself. If I had truly loved myself and realized that I WAS love, then what they did on their journey wouldn't have affected me, even if it was aimed at me.

Today I don't draw in manipulative people. I have the most amazing, beautiful people around me because I know that I am love; I'm not looking for it. Even if someone does show up in my life in a not-so-nice way, it doesn't affect me in a negative way. I just ask myself, *Oh, Kelly, what did you draw this person in for? What are you supposed to be learning here?* I become the necessary narcissist, looking inside at myself first, and then I let that person's projection stay theirs. They are doing what they are doing because that is where they are at in their journey of learning. If someone truly understands that they are love, and love who they are, there is absolutely no desire to project hurt, wounding, judgment or criticism onto others, so I don't need to take what they do personally.

Everyone here on this Earth is living their own journey with their own set of unique reactionary needs, triggers, behaviors and emotional drivers. When they judge you, project their insecurity or anger onto you or blame you, all they are really doing is reacting to you based on their own personal sense of self-worth. It may look like, smell like or even taste like they are reacting to you, but realistically they are just reacting to themselves and their own human conditioning; you don't need to take it personally or engage with it. When you are on your own journey of healing and someone collides with your journey emotionally or mentally, stay the internal narcissist. Separate from the needs of the ego. Don't look at their behavior, even if they are hopping mad, saying hurtful things, projecting their own hurt onto you, stating a non-truth, blaming you or are reciting a laundry list of what you did wrong. They can lob an angry hate ball at you all they want, but you don't need to catch it.

During the dissolution stage it is important to turn inside and recognize when you are triggering based on your own human conditioning. Once you master looking inside first, then you can see what still needs to be healed within you and you can clearly see the ego at work.

It is also important to understand that

EGO = FEAR

Ego is trying to get you to look for love and acceptance outside of yourself and for a sense of self-worth through others' belief that you are important. This creates fear of rejection, betrayal, not being good enough, not being successful enough, not being seen well by others mentally, emotionally and physically. This fear causes jealousy, resentment, hurt, wounding, rejection, judgment, projection, hate, depression, shame, guilt, and a need for power and control.

The systems in our society are a product of this fear and are an attempt to keep the ego alive in it's striving for importance, power and control (see figure 11).

Ego Flowchart

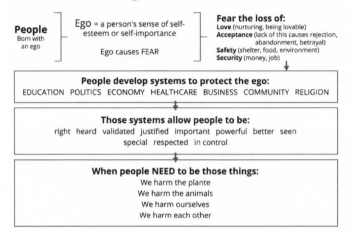

Figure II

The ego also wants you to believe you are separate from everything and separate from Source. As a consequence there is a feeling that you are not safe. My Guides have explained that there is no safe or unsafe, just a manifestation of what is going on inside of you. You are drawing all situations to you based on your heart-code, so the only *unsafe* is you. I know that if I am not in fear of being physically harmed, I am not going to have that in my life unless it is something I need to learn on my journey; and, in that case, bring it on!

In this time of necessary narcissistic ego exposure, continuously reflect on your fears and ask yourself what it is you fear about you. Do you fear you are not enough? Do you fear you are not loved? Do you fear you won't have enough? Keep it internal and look for the opportunity for further healing. Continue to recognize and heal the ego so that the authentic you can be separated from the ego.

The authentic you is who you truly are as a being, whether that is gentle, sensitive, intuitive, creative, fiery, curious, deep or quiet. It is you free from need for acceptance, attention, validation or approval from others. It is just you at your core. Many people who have been buried by human conditioning for so long have no idea who this person is. They might see glimpses of their authentic self in their younger selves, usually before age thirteen, before their human conditioning took over, but they have forgotten how to be that person. This time of separation is a time to allow the beautiful traits, qualities and characteristics of your soul-you to shine through. This is a time to be empowered to be you, however that looks, and love and own your uniqueness.

For me, my authentic me is being courageously clairvoyant. I came out of the psychic closet years ago and I have no interest in going back in. My Guides told me early on that I would be teaching some unconventional understandings about life and many of them may cause me to be rejected, criticized, disbelieved and even shunned. They asked me if I still wanted to go through with being a teacher in this manner and I instantly said, "Yes!" I don't want to live a façade' of lies because I fear that people will think I am weird, unbalanced, quirky or just plain crazy. I am who I am and when we separate from the ego, being normal is just not important anymore.

At a party once, I was standing around with a group of men who were asking me what I did for a living. I shared that I was clairvoyant and was in the healing arts field. They seemed intrigued, but one gentleman was looking at me with a very perplexed look on his face. He eventually said, "How do you date? I mean, aren't you reading everyone all the time? I don't think I could handle someone knowing what goes on inside of me all of the time." I laughed a little at this, not at him, but inside of me, as I explained that I was actually the best person to date because I do indeed read everyone around me. I see that all of us are working through hurt, wounding, insecurities, rejection, fear and need for control. We are all so vastly unique and our vain attempts at conformity are a big fat lie. I told him, "I get to see the authentic you, inside of you, who is beautiful in all of his failings, passions, hurt, uniqueness and vulnerabilities. No one on this life is free from the human condition and no one is like anyone else; we're all just a bunch of human conditioned weirdos. Yeah, I'm the best person to date because you only have to be you around me."

Take this stage of recognizing and separating from your ego-self as a time to let the real you shine. Be gentle with yourself and impregnate your personality with a shot of joy for who you are. Lift yourself out of the quagmire of your broken ego-self and recognize your unborn self. Move through the birth canal into a new, authentic, self-loving you.

Summary of the Separation Stage

- This is the stage where you separate from the ego
- Learn to recognize the ego when it presents itself in the form of keeping you looking for acceptance, love, self-worth and importance outside of yourself
- Watch the ego as though it is a separate part of you who you are taming by deprogramming its desire to keep you stuck in the human condition
- Become the necessary narcissist and keep your focus inward, not on what other people are projecting toward you due to their own hurt and wounded human conditioned self
- Allow your authentic self to surface and shine as the unique you that you are

Chapter four
Conjunction
Union

Our life is made up of opposites—good and bad, beautiful and ugly, right and wrong, positive and negative, masculine and feminine—when we can appreciate the value at both ends, the sweet balance of the center is just a heartbeat away

---

Reminder of the Alchemical Stages

Stage 1: Calcination:
To convert with heat or burning (human conditioning)

Stage 2: Dissolution:
To undo or break down (heal internal wounding)

Stage 3: Separation:
Breaking apart or letting go (see the ego when it shows up)

Stage 4: Conjunction:
Union (balance your opposites)

Stage 5: Fermentation:
Change (Dark night of your soul and golden light)

Stage 6: Distillation:
Purification (let go of old habits and safety zones)

Stage 7: Coagulation:
To change into a thicker, stronger mass

When I was growing up back in the late 1970's and early 1980's there was an awesome Saturday morning cartoon series called "Schoolhouse Rock" that taught grammar, math, history, science and politics through super memorable songs like, "Unpack your Adjectives" "Interplanet Janet" and

"I'm just a Bill"; they were great! One of my favorites was called "Conjunction Junction" and one of the verses in the song is:

Conjunction Junction, what's your function?
Hooking up phrases and clauses that balance, like:
Out of the frying pan and into the fire.
He cut loose the sandbags,
But the balloon wouldn't go any higher.
Let's go up to the mountains,
Or down to the sea.
You should always say "thank you",
Or at least say "please".

The night before I was to write this chapter, I asked my Guides to give me inspiration for explaining the Conjunction stage. I woke up the next morning singing the "Conjunction Junction" song, something I hadn't thought about in years. It's a hilarious tune that is kind of like jazz funk meets show tune musical. Anyway, after irritatingly looping the same verse over and over in my head a trillion times it finally hit me that I was singing about the word Conjunction—I'm a little slow in the morning. I laughed because I had asked for inspiration and realized that is what my Guides brought me! Really? I'm writing a book about alchemy and their inspiration is "Hookin' up words and phrases and clauses!" Have I told you that my Guides have a great sense of humor?

Since I couldn't stop the lyrical loop in my head, and was sure I was butchering the words, I looked them up. Of course, I immediately saw that there was a perfect correlation between the song and this alchemical stage. The song is talking about using conjunctions "and", "but" or "or" to either unify sentences or words, or bring them together in a grammatically balanced way. Imagine the fourth stage of alchemy, Conjunction, to be much like these lyrics are explaining. These conjunctions, "and", "but" and "or" join ideas together in a balanced way, which is what this stage is all about—joining together two ways of being, or two concepts about life, in a balanced way. It is bringing about internal union.

The word conjunction also means the action of two or more things occurring at the same point in time and space, coming together in balance. As humans, we have so many opposite ways of existing and perceiving that are playing themselves out in the same space and time here on Earth, and the Conjunction stage of alchemy is when we bring these opposites into balance.

In traditional alchemy, the Conjunction stage is where the alchemist recombines the saved, or separated, elements left over after the first three alchemical stages—Calcination, Dissolution and Separation—to produce a new substance. The alchemists are producing, out of the opposing elements of fire in Conjunction, water in Dissolution and air in Separation, a new compound, earth, in the Conjunction phase. In other words, they are bringing about a balanced new union by bringing together opposing elements.

Often this was a forced union done by fusing or amalgamating metals or by mixing saved components in a new chemical reaction. The alchemist achieved this forced union by adding in another substance, such as an acid, to accelerate the chemical reaction. In your own being, the Conjunction stage is your union of your opposing ways of being or existing to create a more balanced you. You too will add in another

101

substance such as anger, frustration, exhaustion, or some other emotionally acidic accelerator that causes you to shift into balance.

For me this acidic accelerator showed up as anger. In my early years, before the age of eight, I had pretty feminine energy about me. I was open, loving, intuitive, free-spirited, playful and loved to snuggle. After that age, when I chose to make my intuition my flaky secret, I became internally angry. As a result, I moved into the masculine energies of being in my head, analyzing what people thought of me, and compartmentalizing within me how the world was harsh, critical and hard. This masculine way of being continued to grow as I developed more and more calcification, or life-burning human conditioning, and as a result became controlling and forceful. Yes, I was loving and kind too, but I had built up a lot of internal resentment that came out as anger. It was by no accident that every door jam on our family home was broken from my angrily slamming doors as hard as I could. I now can't help but smile and shake my head as I recall my father often yelling to me as I was about to stomp off in some repetitive huff about who knows what, "There she goes! Stomp-stomp-wiggle-wiggle-slam!" He was referring to my stomping feet, angrily wiggling hips and indignant slamming of a door that was the inevitable outlet for my anger. Well, that and some vicious words I would spit out at whoever would hear. I have to give my dad credit; he said to my mother one time that the things that were making me a really shitty teenager were going to make me a great adult. He couldn't have been more right, but it took me a long time to realize that. At that time I used my anger as a defense against the "mean" life I was living in. Subconsciously I believed that if I stayed in control and forced away anything I didn't like in life, I was safe and couldn't be hurt.

My anger calmed down by the time I entered adulthood, but it still surfaced here and there when my hurt or insecurity was triggered; it was my go-to defense mechanism. This changed significantly after moving through my third alchemy stage, the Separation stage, and I rarely saw it. Oh, what a peaceful time that was! Well, peaceful until I entered my Conjunction stage. When I was ready to heal my masculine imbalance and all of the force and control that was my deep-rooted safety net, my anger surfaced quite a bit. This was like the acid, or acidic accelerator, that traditional alchemists used to force or accelerate chemical change of a substance. For me, my anger was the accelerator and it was going to force me to change.

The beginning of this stage was a difficult one for me because I had been in such a great place for so long. When the anger resurfaced, I actually thought I had regressed in my growth. During this time my anger-acid would blast people when I was challenged or criticized. At the time I didn't realize it, but this was so perfect. It was perfect because I had moved into such a place of self-love and appreciation for life, that I was able to be internally shaken when this anger reaction surfaced. I remember a close friend saying to me that when my anger was triggered, I looked like I was a crazy person. I felt crazy. And thank goodness I did, because that anger surfacing, and my reactionary triggers displaying themselves in such an uncharacteristic manner, are what catapulted me into change. I disliked my own reaction so vehemently that I was forced to look at the imbalance between my gentle, compassionate way of being and my controlling, forceful way of being. It became blatantly obvious to me that I needed balance between my masculine and feminine energies. Because so much of my life and way of being had moved into such a healthy place, internally and externally, this contrast of behavior stuck out like a sore thumb and demanded my attention.

When you enter this stage of Conjunction, do not be surprised if you have old reactions, habits, fears or behaviors that surface. Have no fear, I say with a wink, this is just your acidic accelerator! You are not slipping back, you are being provided with two things:

1. The opportunity to heal old conditioning within you at an even deeper level; peeling a deeper layer of the onion
2. The opportunity to see and address within you opposing ways of being that are in need of balancing

The main opposites of the human existence that come together in the Conjunction stages are:

Masculine and feminine energy
Left and right brain
External force and internal strength
Pituitary gland and pineal gland
Giving and receiving

Remember that by the time you get ready to master the Conjunction stage, you will have already:

1. Been burned by your human conditioning in the **Calcination stage**

2. Broken down the false beliefs and emotional drivers that were not working within you by healing your younger "yous" in the **Dissolution stage**
3. Broken apart from or let go of much of the control of the ego in the **Separation stage**

You will have revealed, or rebirthed a new you that reflects more of your authentic personality. You will be living in a more healed space of self-love, compassion and tolerance for yourself and others. You will understand this world to be a classroom and will have come to peace with what the ego is teaching you. You will appreciate those blasted hard lessons you have gone through time and again throughout the first three alchemical stages. It is at this point you are ready to bring balance to your new expanded you.

Remember that you are actually learning about and going through all alchemical stages simultaneously, learning little by little in each stage. So you may have experienced bringing some balance to yourself over time. However, you cannot master this stage until you have mastered the first three.

It may seem like a lot has to happen before getting to mastery of this stage, but do not allow yourself to feel overwhelmed or think that you are miles away from this stage. I have watched people move into this stage fairly quickly because they were ready to move and shift their inner self. When you are ready to move, you will, and if you are not ready, consider it perfect because you will stay in the place you are at until you amass enough mistakes, successes and experiences that will allow you to be ready. There is no race to alchemizing you, it happens in perfect timing. Just by reading this book, becoming aware of where you can go and motivating yourself for change, you will move on your journey to one extent or another. And when you are ready you will naturally move into the Conjunction stage. As is the case with all of the stages of alchemy, you will move into this stage without being conscious you are doing so. It just happens.

During this time, the overarching concept in need of balancing is that of masculine and feminine energy. If you understand these two opposing types of energy you will understand the premise of all of the other opposites to balance. When I speak of masculine, I am not referring to a man specifically, and when I speak of feminine, I am not speaking about a woman specifically. However, there is a generality about male and female behavior that does relate to the masculine and feminine energies. I get a little twitchy when I speak about masculine and feminine because some people think that referencing it is placing one gender as better or worse than the other, and that is just not the case. Because of this male/female bias, in my online classroom I attempted to teach this concept using the word "flowy" meaning feminine energy and "crunchy" meaning masculine energy, and explained that we were working to achieve "flowchy." It just didn't fly, so I went back to the traditional masculine and feminine descriptors. Oh well, I tried!

Masculine energy is mental, logical, compartmentalized, structured, externally forceful, often domineering, and centered in control. Feminine energy is emotional, creative, free flowing, unstructured, internally strong, intuitive, and centered in wisdom. Most people operate with a propensity toward one or the other, causing varying levels of imbalance within them. Existing in either of these energies without equal balance from the other will result in unhealthy thought, behavior and emotions. Both masculine and feminine energies are valuable, should be seen as such, and require balance for you to be operating from an authentically peaceful place within you.

To begin explaining the process of working through the Conjunction stage, I am using the Balancing Masculine & Feminine chart (figure 12) to explain masculine and feminine energy, left and right brain and external force and internal power. I've chosen these specific three because they are so closely interrelated and constantly affect one another.

In this chart you can see how the masculine brain, masculine power and masculine energies are all fairly similar in their behavior and function, just as the feminine energy, brain and power are all similar in their behavior and function. Each side of this chart has necessary qualities for us to function well in life, but operating from one side without the balance of the other leads to overall imbalance as a being, and consequently in life.

Balancing Masculine & Feminine		
	Centered in the Masculine	Centered in the Feminine
Energy	• Brain Chatter • Structured • External force • Solar plexus is power center • Ego-centered • Serious	• Wisdom • Fluid • Internal strength • Heart is power center • Love-centered • Playful • Intuitive
Brain	**Left Brain** • Directed • Closed-minded Linear • Analytical • Practical Organizational Logical • Black & white • Compartmentalized • No-nonsense	**Right Brain** • Creative • Random • Open-minded Expressive Emotional Passionate • Holistic • Free-spirited Kinesthetic • Artistic
Power	**External Force** • Forcing something to happen • Control • Power over someone or something • Removing all barriers • Ego-based	**Internal Strength** • Trusting • Manifesting • Internal knowing • Acting upon when presented with inspiration or opportunity • Letting life unfold

Figure 12

A Side Note About Masculine and Feminine Energies

The father in figure 15 represents masculine traits and mother represents feminine traits. Historically, the father, or masculine traits, have been referred to as blades and the mother, or feminine traits, as chalices. This may seem familiar if you understand traditional tarot, because in the cards the blades are referred to as swords, which have to do with the mental aspects of the self and the chalice is referred to as cups, which have to do with the emotional aspects of the self. Blades are considered masculine not only for the phallic representation that gives the seed of life, but also because it commands power and has the action of external strength. The feminine is referred to as a chalice, representing a cup that holds water, which symbolizes emotion, and an internal strength. This chalice is also considered a vessel of life, biologically a receiver of the male blade and seed, where it holds the creation of life, a womb. It is no secret that throughout history women, the mother, typically operate from their emotional side and men, the father, typically operate from their mental side. This is not saying that all men are mental and all women are emotional, this figure is just using the gender reference to signify a type of behaving. The time is now for these two energies and ways of being to balance within ourselves as well as humanity as a whole.

Left and Right Sides of Body

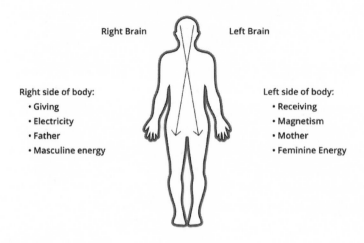

Right Brain   Left Brain

Right side of body:
- Giving
- Electricity
- Father
- Masculine energy

Left side of body:
- Receiving
- Magnetism
- Mother
- Feminine Energy

Figure 13

The *Left and Right Sides of the Body* figure helps to explain this even further (see figure 13). The figure indicates that the right, feminine brain operates the left side of the body and the left, masculine brain operates the right side of the body. Notice how the right side of the body, masculine, is electricity, which can be viewed as externally forceful and the left side, feminine, is magnetism, which can be viewed as attracting or drawing toward you. These are two different ways of behaving in life and both have their place. However, too much of one, without balance from the other is not healthy. Think of it like this, manifesting, or drawing to you what you desire, without grounded logic can be as unbalanced as forcing something to happen without flowing in harmony with what life is offering. It is not any more healthy to continuously force life to happen by pushing and controlling outcomes than it is to sit around the pool popping Bonbon's flippantly saying, "I'm manifesting!"

waiting for life to show up for you. There is healthy balance in being internally reflective, listening intuitively and staying positive while also doing hard work, organizing and moderately planning; this is balanced masculine and feminine at work.

If you look at the *Left and Right Sides of the Body* figure again (figure 13), you can see that the masculine right side involves "giving", which is externally moving something away from you (masculine electric force) and the left side involves "receiving" which is internally accepting something for yourself (internal magnetic attraction). These two opposites must balance each other out. You don't want to give so much that you are not taking care of yourself, just as you don't want to take too much from others in a selfish, over-indulging, or disempowering way. You need to have equal balance with giving and receiving that is not needs based. Many people need to feel better about themselves by giving, causing them to over give, just as there are people who place themselves in a place of lack or don't feel empowered to achieve on their own so they feel a need to take from others or the system. Our giving and receiving, forcing and attracting, making it happen and manifesting all need to be in balance with each other or our way of existing in this life will consistently bring about imbalanced results.

One of the major imbalances of our society right now is the over-valuing of and over-indulgence in masculine traits. We can see this in all of our major systems—political, mercantile, economic, environmental, agricultural, and educational. For example, we teach logic, memory, calculation and problem-solving in schools, which are all masculine energy traits, but it is not balanced with an EQUAL value for or formal teaching of

111

uncovering personal creativity and passions, understanding feelings, social interaction, understanding mental conflict, listening to an inner voice, learning to relax, and healthy self-talk, which are all feminine energy traits. Think about the importance of having this balance. Our school system was created to develop healthy, productive members of our communities. However, how can we be healthy and ethically productive if we are only educating in the mind? Healthy people are also balanced in their emotions, creative expression, social interactions, and behavior.

It's not just in the school system where you can see an imbalance. You can witness an unhealthy desire for power, importance and control, which are derived from masculine traits, in all systems. You can see this through the actions of valuing money over love, profit over animals and our earth, need for dominance of property and political boarders over compassion and collaboration. Thankfully, as more and more of us begin to understand our own personal internal balance of masculine and feminine, our society will begin to reflect this balance as well.

To further understand how to balance the masculine and feminine energies, the male and female brain, internal and external power and the different sides of the body, I am going to explain the balancing of the pituitary gland and pineal gland. This, at first, may seem a random way to explain balancing of your opposites, but these glands are so steeped in the masculine and feminine that they are really the key to balancing the others.

The pituitary and pineal glands are both located in the head and are part of the endocrine system, a collection of glands in the body that release the hormones and chemicals needed to regulate bodily functions like metabolism or sleep. The pituitary gland is located behind the bridge of your nose in front of where the spinal cord attaches to the brain and the pineal gland is in the center of your head behind where the spinal cord attaches (see figure 14).

Pineal and Pituitary Glands

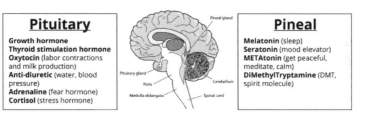

Figure 14

These two glands release chemicals and hormones in the endocrine system that relate to your happy and fearful states of being. The pituitary gland releases your growth hormone when you are young, it stimulates the thyroid gland, it releases Oxytocin in women for labor contractions and milk production, and it releases an anti-diuretic in the body, which are all needed. But the pituitary gland also releases the fear-based chemicals of adrenaline, the fight or flight hormone, and cortisol, the stress hormone. Opposing the fearful

113

chemicals, the pineal gland releases chemicals that produce a more happy response in the body. It releases melatonin so you can sleep, serotonin the mood elevator, and it is theorized that DiMethylTryptamine, also known as DMT, is released here. DMT is one of the ingredients found in METAtonin, which is said to allow you to get peaceful and meditate. We need both of these glands to be in good function and in balance with each other. Think of it like this, if our brains were drunk on METAtonin, we would get so peaceful we'd just sit around in a happy box doing nothing but flashing a complacent peace sign; whereas, if we had too much adrenaline floating around in our bodies we'd schitz out like a paranoid junkie. We need a little fear in our being so that we don't do something stupid, like walk in front of a bus just as much as we need peace and serenity to allow us to take time to sit in our own stillness.

Because these two glands are in the head, they are affected by our thinking. One of the things my Guides shared with me early on in working with clients, and something I have seen come to truth time and again, is that we need to work on our mental beliefs first before trying to heal a broken emotion within the body. It is what is in your mental chatter that will keep a negative or positive emotion alive and able to heal or not. Along that same line, we need to balance the mind's functioning in order to balance the rest of our opposites. We need to adjust where our thinking is centered before we are able to bring balance to our masculine and feminine energies.

Not all of what I am going to explain next has evidence in scientific research; some of it has been channeled through me. This information has been explained by my Guides time and again so, for me, is truth. However, you will have to reach inside of you and ask yourself whether or not this information resonates with you to be held as your own truth. Well, I say with a playful grin, "That is until science catches up with my Guides and shows otherwise."

Having said that, there is, and has been, a lot of research conducted around the pineal gland, consciousness, DMT and its effect on our thoughts, feelings, spirituality and personal growth. If you are so inclined to read more about this fascinating research I am going to point you toward D. B. Barrett of Asheville, NC and his brilliant article called The Pineal Gland and the Chemistry of Consciousness, referenced at the end of this book. The article compiles research conducted around this topic and helps to make insightful connections between separate bodies of information. It also includes what I call the bonus of all bonuses; at the end of the article he provides you links to forty plus resources of information about research and theory around this subject that can keep your nose to paper with "What the!" "Are you kidding?" and "Holy hell!" exclamations for a very long time.

What my Guides have explained about the pituitary gland is that when you are continuously in your masculine thinking, your energy of thought is centered in the brain's frontal cortex (forehead area). The frontal cortex has to do with emotional reaction, problem solving, logic, reasoning, memory, language, judgment and analytical thinking. This is a beautiful, needed part of our brain. However, when you center your thought in this area in excess, or without balance from your feminine thinking, you continuously trigger the release of cortisol, the stress hormone and adrenaline, the fear hormone. This, in turn, causes a vicious cycle of toxic fearful stress chemicals in the body, which then keeps your mind in perpetual chatter, which then releases more adrenaline and cortisol—it's a vicious cycle.

When your thought is centered in the pineal gland, also known as your third eye, you are in open-minded thinking; open to receive inspiration, creativity, clarity, wisdom and intuitive guidance. The pineal gland is complex and has been mentioned as a sacred symbol throughout history, in cultures around the world. I can tell you that in my early years when I didn't know anything about the pineal gland, my Guides began speaking about and directed me to center my thinking there in order to hear them more clearly, understand universal wisdom and knowledge, and be in a calm, loving space. However, what they also told me is that if you remain there without balance from the masculine thinking of the frontal cortex, you will not be grounded in your approach to this life and you can easily become flighty or unrealistic.

After my first initial clearing in the second stage of Dissolution, I was in such a place of love. I had never felt so good and didn't want to leave that euphoric feeling. For about a month I flitted around going, "Love! Oh, Love! This is lovely! That is lovely! Isn't it all lovely, lovely?" Oh good Lord. I remember saying to myself, *Ok, Kell, you need to ground, honey. You are not going to do anything productive with this loving way of being if you don't get back on Earth and get real!* I needed balance from my masculine energies to make the love I was experiencing something I could bring to this world with any reality.

Speaking of reality, you know how so many mystical pictures show an eye painted on the forehead or in the center of the head. Well, I hate to burst any spiritual bubbles, but it's not really so mystical at all. The pineal gland is a hollow, fluid-filled gland that has photoreceptors just like the retina of your eye, which is why it is referred to as a *third* eye. To understand the function of the pineal, outside of releasing happy, Zen-like chemicals into your body, you need to first understand how the eyes you see with work. Your eyes see a projected image in front of you because light and energy enter into the retina's photoreceptors at different vibrations, or wavelengths. What happens as a result, in basic understanding, is that lower vibrations of this energy that enter the eyes will be seen as colors like reds and oranges and higher vibrations will be seen as colors like indigo and violet. These vibrations are creating a visual language in your eyes and projecting an image of distance, light and dark, and color in the form of sight.

The pineal gland is an eye in that it has photoreceptors like the retina of your eyes. But the question you may have is what are you doing with the ability to create sight in the center of your head? What my Guides have explained is this; the pineal gland has energy that enters in from the temples located at the sides of the head, the area a Bindi would be located, in the center of the forehead above the eyebrows, which a skull fissure called the glabella, and the soft spots of the head also known as the skull's anterior and posterior fontanels on the top and back of the crown of the head (see figure 15).

Energy Openings into Pineal gland

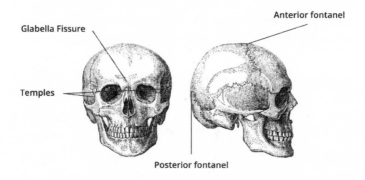

Figure 15

The energy that enters into those areas meet in the pineal gland. What my Guides have explained is that this energy vibration carries with it information, or a language; much like the color-language your eyes see. This is also known as clairvoyance, psychic knowing or intuitiveness. This psychic-language is no less real than our sight-language. I've asked my Guides why, if we all have this gland, people don't all have awareness of their intuition?

They explained that it is because too many people get so trapped in chatter, worry, fear and analytical thinking that they cannot hear their own psychic-language. They also explained that clairvoyance is like an athletic ability. Most of us have arms and can throw a ball, but not all of us are going to be the star quarterback. Certainly not me; whenever I attempt to throw a snowball it usually splats the ground in front of me causing the intended target to be forced to hide a snicker ladled with *oh you poor thing* pathetic eyes. In that same aspect, we all have a pineal gland but it may not be as developed in some people as it is in others. I may stink at throwing, but imagine, if you will, Saturday Night Live's Molly-Shannon striking her best "Superstar!" pose as I say I like to think of myself as a, "Clairvoyant Superstar!"

My Guides have explained that anyone can strengthen their psychic-language even if they are not the "Superstar". They said to consider the pineal gland to be like a muscle. Just like when you go to the gym and work out your muscles to become stronger, if you work out your pineal gland, your psychic abilities will also become stronger. So how do you do that? By learning to becomes aware of where your conscious thought is resting in your brain and then noticing where it is projecting. Based on where you project your awareness, you will be able to perceive different aspects of yourself and the world outside of you. When my Guides first had me move around in my head in this way it felt like I was "clicking" into each place, so I personally like to call this movement the "clicks of the pineal" (see figure 16).

Clicks of the Pineal

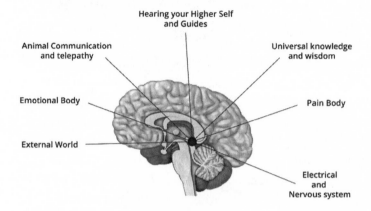

Hearing your Higher Self
and Guides

Animal Communication
and telepathy

Universal knowledge
and wisdom

Emotional Body

Pain Body

External World

Electrical
and
Nervous system

Figure 16

The key to understanding this pineal movement is to learn what it feels like to have your conscious thought centered in the pineal gland. To do this you need to move your conscious thought out of your brain's frontal cortex, or forehead area. What you need to do is close your eyes and notice where your conscious thought is resting. If it is in the front of your head, by the forehead, imagine surrendering all of your thought and floating your attention back behind your eyes into the center of your head. If it bounces out and wants to go back to the forehead, just recognize its desire to be in control, send it a little internal love and let it float back to the center again. When your conscious thought is centered in the pineal gland you are not in brain chatter, analytical thinking or problem solving of any kind. You are just existing in a place of awareness. You are not thinking, you are aware. It feels like you can "see" 360 degrees in all directions at once from inside of yourself because you are in total awareness of yourself, your world around you and your higher wisdom all at once.

Once you learn to get into the pineal and reside there without thought, you can begin to "click" around. To click around imagine that you are centered in the pineal gland and that you have a ray of consciousness that is being directed out of the head. In the graphic, "Pineal Gland Navigation", you can see that when you project your awareness straight up you are able to communicate with your higher self and Guides. Just one click behind there is universal knowledge and wisdom. This is the place where we hear universal truth, wisdom and knowledge or what is considered to be collective conscious thought and understanding. If you click back from there you will be in awareness of your pain body, or where your conscious awareness is located if you are in physical pain, and back from there is your electrical or nervous awareness which is directly related to your pain body.

If you go back to center, where you direct your attention out of the top of your head and click just in front of it, you will have awareness of telepathy, which includes animal communication. In front of that is where your conscious thought goes when it is aware of your emotions and in front of that is where your awareness goes when you are projecting out into the world, onto others or are engaged in the role of the ego.

By clicking around in these areas, you will strengthen your pineal gland and the awareness you have of where your thought is focusing, or projecting. Once you can recognize where your thought is residing, you will then have the ability to consciously bring it back to center.

How Do You Communicate with God?

A lot of people want to know where they hear God. God (also known as Source energy or unconditional love energy) is felt and heard in both the "Higher Self and Guides" and "Universal Knowledge and Wisdom" areas combined, as referenced in the *Clicks of the Pineal graphic* (see figure 16). Imagine centering in the pineal gland and then opening up to those two "clicks" together; kind of like you are opening a sun roof in those two areas. Then open your heart-brain and gut-brain and listen with your whole being. Your pineal gland is like a satellite, receiving information. Once it is open to receive, listen with your internal wisdom, feelings in the heart and gut knowing all at once. The trick is surrendering thought, being calm and centered, and listening with all of you, not just your head. You may see images or colors, hear, taste, smell or just get an unquestionable knowing. We are all unique in how we receive communication, so be open to whatever comes to you.

So that leads to the question, what is center and why bring it back there? "Center" is actually a combination of awareness of the top three "clicks"—connection to your higher self and Guides, universal wisdom and telepathy. I like to imagine the top of my head open so that I have access to all of these areas at once. This whole top-of-the-head opening is what I consider pineal gland or feminine centered thinking. Why do you want to be in this "center" thinking? The pineal gland is like a satellite in that it sends and receives information. What it receives from the center is wisdom and intuition from your higher self, Source, and perceptual awareness around you. If you are focusing your thought out the front of your forehead you are projecting your attention into the outer world, which is good and bad. Good

122

in that it allows you to analyze, problem-solve and plan about life in the outer world, but bad in that it can also cause you to project your internal hurt, wounding and triggers onto others in the outer world. And it can keep you obsessed about worldly things like money, power and control. The best way to balance your conscious thought is to allow it to reside in feminine pineal thinking and only access masculine, pituitary, frontal cortex thinking when needed. Consider the frontal cortex a toolbox with valuable tools of logic, reasoning, sequencing, and problem solving. These are good tools, and we want to have easy access to them, but we don't want to have our thinking reside there. Imagine that if your thought resides there all of the time and rolls around in constant chatter, you are stuck in a dark box full of sharp tools that can cut and do damage. If instead you reside in your pineal centered thought most of the time, you will allow yourself to continuously be open to creativity, inspiration, intuition, wisdom and universal knowledge. The balance comes in when, once you receive inspiration, creativity, or information, you then visit your toolbox, or frontal cortex to problem-solve, calculate, analyze or utilize the rational thought necessary to bring your inspiration into concrete reality.

I know that by keeping myself centered in my pineal, I am in alignment with my higher self, wisdom, inner peace and intuition. I also know that when I am in balance with my masculine and feminine thinking, I am connecting my head-brain, heart-brain and gut brain together so that I am not only in my wisdom, I am compassionate, passionate, and in my internal power and love. And when I am in this place, my frontal cortex, or toolbox, is then not able to throw wrenches of anxiety, fear, over thinking, over analyzing or over planning into the mix. I am in balance.

I explained earlier that the key to balancing your masculine and feminine, and consequently all of your other opposites, is in learning to first balance your pituitary and pineal glands. By balancing where you center your thought, residing in the center of your brain behind the eyes (pineal centered thinking) and accessing the brain's frontal cortex (pituitary centered thinking) as needed you will be operating first from your feminine energies with perfect balance and support from your masculine energies. You will then release more happy pineal gland chemicals through your endocrine system than fear-based pituitary gland chemicals. This will affect how you operate in your power center, allowing you to be internally tenacious. You will be empowered to be the authentic you and a good self-advocate because you are centered in wisdom without using external power and force that come from worry and fear.

By balancing your feminine pineal and masculine pituitary energies, you will value both the left masculine and right feminine brain. As a result, you will have centered, balanced thinking and this will assist you in understanding how to center your power. You will naturally understand that forcing anything to happen out of fear or a need for control is out of balance (imbalanced in masculine thinking). Instead you will operate from an internal place of strength that moves in flow with life. When there is a barrier to whatever it is you are trying to achieve, whether it is in work, relationship, family, society, or as you move through life, you will naturally know not to barrel through it with force, judging those who brought

124

the barrier into your field of perception. Instead you will be like the water that flows toward a rock in the stream. When it hits the rock, it knows there is another way and gracefully moves around it in harmony with nature, not judging the rock for being there or stopping its flow because it came into contact with it. It just simply flows with its own power to stay its course without destruction.

In this place of balanced power you will be a good self-advocate, standing up for yourself when needed in an uneventful, non-dramatic way. You will create mutually respectful boundaries with those around you while honoring their journey as much as your own. You will have the courage to be who you are authentically and feel empowered to be that person without needing anyone else to approve of who you are or follow your lead. And lastly, you will feel empowered to go for your dreams with love and compassion, logic and reason, and grounded inspiration.

You will be open to receive beauty, love, affection, abundance, kindness or assistance when it presents itself to you. You will equally be open to giving from an internal place of compassion as opposed to out of a need to feel better, be in control, feel sorry for, or feel validated by the act of giving. You are in balance with your giving and receiving and are gracious in the actions of both.

The fourth stage of Conjunction cannot be mastered until you complete the other three stages because you need to be in a place of authentic self-love. You need to separate yourself from the ego and its need to be in control, power and importance. And you need to be in a place of feeling that it doesn't matter whether or not you are acknowledged and accepted by others because you love and value yourself. These things are accomplished through the first three stages and have set the stage for your Conjunction stage to bring you into balance. You are now in perfect internal positioning for mastering the next stages of alchemy, Fermentation and distillation.

Summary of the Conjunction Stage

- This is the stage of balancing your opposites:
  - Masculine and feminine energy
  - Left and right brain
  - External force and internal strength
  - Pituitary gland and pineal gland
  - Giving and receiving
- The overarching opposites in need of balancing are your masculine and feminine energies, which affect all other opposites
- The key to balancing masculine and feminine energies is to balance your pineal gland and pituitary gland
- You balance your pineal and pituitary gland by having your thinking centered in the area of your pineal, accessing the pituitary, frontal cortex thinking, as support

---

Chapter five
fermentation
Change

You are just like a flower in that you will blossom most brilliantly when you eagerly dig your roots deep into the pile of manure you are meant to grow out of

Love is a state of being, not an action

Unconditional love means, literally, there are no conditions

Reminder of the Alchemical Stages

Stage 1: Calcination:
To convert with heat or burning (human conditioning)

Stage 2: Dissolution:
To undo or break down (heal internal wounding)

Stage 3: Separation:
Breaking apart or letting go (see the ego when it shows up)

Stage 4: Conjunction:
Union (balance your opposites)

Stage 5: Fermentation:
Change (Dark night of your soul and golden light)

Stage 6: Distillation:
Purification (let go of old habits and safety zones)

Stage 7: Coagulation:
To change into a thicker, stronger mass

I have decided to nominate Darth Vader as our inspiration for this chapter, with his famous words "You underestimate the power of the dark side," defining our overall theme. Stage five of the alchemical process is called Fermentation, and is often referred to as the stage of The Dark Night of Your Soul. I feel like I want to insert a "Muahahaha" Dracula laugh here, but that might be in competition with Darth and I really don't want that drama right now. This stage sounds frightening and ominous I'm sure, but it's actually lighter than you may be thinking. Remember, Darth Vader did come out as good in the end, I mean, well, he was a little veiny and kind of slimy looking, but he was good! Right?

Well, the Fermentation stage can be a little slimy too, so this is a fitting inspiration. This stage comes after an alchemist has brought together the opposing elements from the first three stages of alchemy and has unified these into a new element in the Conjunction stage. He is then ready to bring new life force into the material he has been cultivating since stage one, Calcination. The Fermentation stage has two phases—Putrefaction and Spiritization. Putrefaction is where the good material the alchemist has extracted is left alone to rot and decompose. Most often manure is added to this material to accelerate the rotting process. By adding this, the digesting bacteria from the manure brings new life force into the material. This new life force changes the nature of the material until a milky white fluid accumulates on the blackened, rotting material. Slimy.

The appearance of this milky white substance, often called the "golden wax" of fermentation, signifies that the second phase has begun. This second phase is called Spiritization in that it brings about the spirits or substance to be used in the final two stages of alchemy. This spirit comes out of the foul white slime and its arrival is announced by the formation of an iridescent, oily film alchemists called "Peacock's Tail." This oily ooze is what will eventually become the essential oil or purified material at the end of the alchemical process.

Just as the Fermentation stage has two phases when working with metal, animal or plant, it has two phases when alchemizing you as well. The first phase, Putrefaction, is referred to as The Dark Night of Your Soul and the second, Spiritization, is referred to as The Golden Light. The titles in these phases kind of tell the tale of this stage, but it still requires much explanation, so Darth and I shall continue.

Once you have reached the Fermentation stage of alchemy, you will be in quite a sweet spot within yourself. You will feel happy and loving most of the time, though still experiencing the human condition from time to time. You are in such a place of inner-love and balance that when life shows up, it is easy for you to move through it with grace and ease. Negative people will be very hard for you to be around and they will naturally drop out of your life because their energetic signature is no longer a match with yours. Drama, feeling like a victim, and harsh life lessons are almost non-existent at this point. However, and this is a big however, there is something lurking beneath the surface in a visceral place within you, fermenting and rotting until it is ready to ooze. Don't be scared, this "ooze" is a necessary part of transformation and it will come out of your "golden wax" that allows you to shine more brilliantly than you could ever imagine.

129

The best way for me to explain this is to share my story of Fermentation with you.

You may recall that the four statements that I made about myself as a result of my Calcination stage were, I am a worthless person, I am a bad person, I am sick and I am broken. Thankfully, my Dissolution and Separation stages got rid of these statements, and I moved into a more loving place within me. After that my Conjunction stage allowed me to live a balanced life with a tamed sense of force and external power. I am careful to say "more loving" and "tamed sense" in the sentences prior because I still had some self-love and further taming to bring about within me. This was to occur at such a deep place of inner growth that it could not be realized until I was this far into the alchemical process. It would extract from within me the deepest wounds of my child-self and the deepest lesson I came here to move through.

At the time I hit this stage I was successful in my holistic healing practice, had beautiful people supporting me, and was in a place within myself that felt whole, balanced and loving. However, as I mentioned earlier, in this phase there is something lurking beneath the surface, at a visceral level. This something was fermenting and rotting in my foundation and would eventually need to surface.

Up until this time, loyalty was the most important thing I could ever imagine someone possessing and I held it in such a high place of importance that I could not imagine ever being complete and whole without it being within me and in those around me. I was viciously loyal to the people I let into my heart and could never imagine ever betraying that tight, intimate bond, or them doing it to me.

Since Darth Vader is our inspiration, I will say that although I was feeling like I was in a balanced and loving place at that time, there was a "disturbance in the force" that was gnawing away at me in the background of my mind. My business partner and I were trying to develop a new healthcare model; and although I knew it came out of a beautiful and compassionate vision, something was just not right. We could not get funding and no matter what direction we turned to make things work our efforts were not being supported. Frustrated, I kept saying, "There is a barrier here and I am just not seeing it!" and I truly could not. Not yet.

My business partner was my best friend, my roommate, my confidante, and someone I trusted with all that I was. I believed our loyalty to each other spanned the tests of time, the universe and all of existence. You know when you meet someone and know deep within that you have known that person for lifetimes? Well, that's what it felt like, that we could feel the karmic connection between us at a core level. I will call this person Cameron. I trusted him beyond anything. I trusted him so much so that we started a business together without a contract between us, out of the goodness of our hearts, to do better for the world and all in it. Here is where I insert the skipping record sound. Yes, I know, naive and overly trusting, but give me a break; we met just after I entered the Dissolution stage and my wisdom wasn't completely intact yet. What I didn't know is that Cameron had a big role to play in my life and my life lessons. And although we were indeed connected at a karmic level, it was not in the way I thought. Our karma, or contract to play a

131

role in each other's growth, was to play itself out in the Fermentation stage.

Just a reminder that karma, to me, is not the idea that you have done something wrong so now you will pay, or you have banked enough good so you will get something good in return. Karma, to me, is the understanding that you have life lessons that span lifetimes. Have you learned them? No? Ok, here are more lessons. Or, oh, you have learned them? Ok. You do not need to continue with this lesson any longer so you are free of this repetitive cycle of karmic learning. There are people who are connected to your karma who agreed to play a role for you and that is often the karmic connection we feel when we meet someone. This role they play can be a beautiful or brutal role, but from Source perspective, it all comes out of love.

Cameron was to play a karmic role in my life to bring to me one of my greatest lessons. He was to teach me that I could not be betrayed. Not ever.

Oh, don't get me wrong, Cameron's actions were certainly perceived by me at the time as betrayal. I can hear Darth Vader speaking through Cameron now, "I am altering the deal, pray I do not alter it any further..." as if he is speaking about the day I felt betrayal as I could never have ever imagined feeling it.

The events of that day of betrayal, took me to my knees. It was as though someone had turned me inside out from bone to skin so that I was left with nothing but a raw and exposed exterior and a shattered interior. I could kindly be described by anyone looking in at me as a pathetic, hysterical wreck. I don't care to speak of any specifics around this, for even if I did share the details, no one could really understand what I was feeling inside at that time. I no longer carry a story around it and do not want to recreate one now. All I know is that I was in shock as I fled our home, went to a campground and proceeded to cry and process what had happened for four days.

Creating Stories

Creating stories is when something bad happens, and you feel hurt by someone or a victim to them and have a story to tell about what happened. These stories, whether fact or not, your perception or theirs, will only keep you stuck in the pain. When you create a story of what happened, and feel compelled to tell your tale of hurt, you are not looking internally for personal healing. You are focusing externally, keeping the pain alive. This keeps you in victim status and hands your power over to the main character in your story. Take your power back, drop the story and ask yourself why you brought that experience to you. It is then that you will heal from the pain and move into a place of gratitude for that teacher entering your life.

In the Dissolution stage I had let go of old beliefs about myself that kept me from experiencing self-worth and self-love that were created in the Calcination stage. Once I shifted those beliefs I was able to separate from the ego in the Separation stage, seeing it when it reared its ugly head, and became balanced in how I operated as a being in my Conjunction stage. Once I had mastered these stages I was ready to ferment and ooze. I was about to become a better person, one that would allow me to live a greater sense of purpose and inspire those around me to also become better people. To do this I needed to enter the dark night of my soul. I believe Darth's words here are quite fitting, "Give yourself to the Dark Side. It is the only way you can save your friends."

What was fermenting inside of me was an internal belief that I could be rejected or betrayed because, although I loved who I was, I still sought love and acceptance outside of myself. This desire to acquire love and acceptance outside of myself was now left alone to rot and decompose and what I perceived as a betrayal from Cameron was just the manure I needed to cultivate new life force within me.

At the campground, I meditated, cried, felt sick, meditated and cried some more. However, because I had gone through the previous alchemical stages, I knew that there was a greater purpose to what I was experiencing. I knew that it was not random and that something within me needed healing and change or I would not be experiencing this dramatic of a level of hurt. On the fourth day, my friend Nia called me and said, "Get out of that campground and get over here!" in such a firm yet loving way that, like a zombie, I packed up all of my gear and drove to her Malibu home.

After a hot shower, Nia's shoulder and a good night's sleep I woke feeling ready to move through this dark night. I was ready to transition in whatever way I needed and let go of the pain. That morning I meditated, asking my Guides to let me see the higher purpose of this experience and to allow me to have the inner strength to move through it with grace. With a half smirk, I say that this is where Darth inserts his, "The force is strong in this one." comment. We all have inner strength to pull from and during this time I pulled hard from the passionate side of my internal fire, as opposed to the anger side of my fire, as I had in my Conjunction stage. This was the internal fire that said, *I will persevere no matter what!* During the meditation I heard from my Guides that I was to leave the healing center I had built, leave the home I'd lived in for the last four years, leave the project to change healthcare I initiated. And leave Cameron.

I walked inside, sat on my friend's couch and with a dumbfounded stare told her I was leaving my center and leaving Cameron. And when asked what I was going to do, I remember issuing a disbelieving laugh while also feeling that I knew everything would be ok and saying, "I don't know but I know it's all going to be ok. And there is this book..." and it is here that I released my golden wax.

Before I go on, know that the book I was talking about at that moment had nothing to do with alchemy, that I knew of. I had a lot of oozing to do before I knew I was writing anything like what you are reading here, but I did feel I was going to write a book eventually. That monumental moment was ten months prior to me realizing that I was to write *this* book, and honestly, I'd forgotten all about it until writing this now.

The reason the book comment was so uneventful in my memory is because of what came next. After I uttered the words, "I don't know but there is this book..." I felt this powerful, warm energy wash over me from right to left. I started to gasp over and over again as I felt it intensely flow into me.

All I could feel was the joy and bliss that had suddenly overtaken me. And at that moment I knew that everything would indeed be okay. In an instance I saw that I had so much to do and so many people to reach with the messages that my Guides have been bringing through me since I was a child. I no longer felt any pain, sadness or sense of betrayal about what had happened. Well, not at that moment anyway.

For the next few days it was like I was in a waking dream. Whatever had washed over me had taken all of my pain away and I was manifesting a new home, money, new clients and a vision for a different future as though I was moving at the speed of light. Envision Han Solo yelling a stellar war cry as he defiantly outruns the Storm Troopers! Yup, that is about how I felt at that moment: creating a whole new future and birthing a whole new me.

Remember how I said that the alchemist added manure so that the bacteria can create a new life force out of the good material created in the former stages of alchemy? That is precisely what had happened. I had created "good material" inside of me that was happy, balanced and self-loving, but that good material had not reached it purist state yet. At this point there were still three more stages of alchemy to go. I had a false belief still inside of me, stemming from my human conditioning. This was a deep-rooted belief, developed by my child-me, that I needed people's acceptance, love and approval. Deep inside of me I believed that I needed that from others to be complete within myself.

The euphoric joy and bliss that washed over me on Nia's couch did wear off after a few days, but the knowing that all would be okay and that I was birthing a new me remained. In alchemy, out of the golden wax an oily film starts to ooze and for the next five months I oozed. Although I was able to keep a positive attitude and use my higher wisdom in all that came my way, I still went through stages of being angry, indignant, victimized, hurt and sad. I mourned the loss of my friend and this emotion needed addressing.

As I was learning where I was going to live long-term and rebuilding my life, I first lived with my friend, Catherine, in her mother-in-law suite. While there, her water main burst, spewing sewage in the area of the house I was staying, ruining her hardwood floors. While she was repairing the pipes and floor I stayed at my friend Pamela's house. Shortly after, her water main also broke. I then moved to a more permanent location, a spa that had a suite for rent, and when I got there the water main broke in my suite, spewing sewage into my room ruining the hardwood floors. I don't believe in coincidence, but regardless, anyone who did would see that this would have been quite the fantastical coincidence to have three water mains break in each of the places I'd stayed. In the world of symbolism water equals emotion and foundations are the foundation within you. Well, if I looked at this literally, my emotional shit was ruining my foundation. My attempts to remain positive were only forcing the emotion down causing a pressure cooker of repressed sadness inside of me that would eventually have to explode. I loved the feeling of bliss I had felt in Malibu so much that I kept trying to recreate it. But not dealing with the sadness I felt head on was allowing it to rot my foundation. I always say our external experiences are a reflection of how we are feeling internally, and I finally forced myself to see what I was manifesting around me. After one of my friends told me I couldn't come over until I was done bursting pipes, I relented and promptly sought out grief counseling.

Throughout the next four months I went through my ups and downs with Cameron, as some of the perceived betrayal continued but each jab attempted didn't land. As my oil oozed from my golden wax I learned, little by little, that this experience was of my own creation and I couldn't resent Cameron. This was not an easy realization though because, despite my best wise-woman self-talk, I really wanted to be the victim. I wanted to blame, point fingers; tell others how bad of a person I thought he was. But internally I didn't believe that. I knew what the experience was about and why it presented itself in my life. It was teaching me and allowing me to grow at the deepest level possible. I actually remember one morning reflecting on how much I had learned and grown that I equated it to giving birth to a child. My daughter Elisabeth took forty-two hours of labor to get out and it was the most grueling, painful experience I'd ever had. But, as most mothers will tell you, I'd do it all over again in a heartbeat to have the amazingness that came out in the end, her. I told my Guides, *I get it. I am in such gratitude for what I have learned; I'd do this again if it means I can learn in this extensive of a way each time.* Remember a little while back when I said, "Be careful what you wish for." About ten minutes later a very nasty hate mail came to my inbox as a result of the situation with Cameron. I felt that internal stab of rejection and looked to my Guides, saying, *I didn't mean now! A little break please!* That stab told me I wasn't quite done oozing.

As the days went on I healed more and more and was finally ready to shift. I more and more understood that Cameron played his role here perfectly, and I believe I consequently brought him opportunity for growth as well. I can only presume he viewed me as someone who likewise rejected him, but that is his tale to tell, not mine. Insert Darth: "Impressive. Most impressive. Obi-Wan has taught you well. You have controlled your fear. Now, release your anger. Only your hatred can destroy me."

Yes, my anger at Cameron did subside, but my oil had one last drop to ooze out and it was one concentrated painful drop. Cameron has a twin; I will call Evan. I knew Evan first and loved him equally as much as I had loved Cameron. I remember the first night I met him he told me, "It's like I've known you for all of my lifetimes!" Yes, we too had karma to experience together. He was the one who brought me to Cameron and he would be the one to help me release my golden light.

Throughout the Cameron experience, Evan stopped talking to me out of loyalty to his brother. I understood that but it didn't make it any less painful for me to receive his silence. Every unanswered text, or lack of communication was one more heart-breaking opportunity to move into my higher self and move away from feeling betrayed, rejected or hurt. I thought I was doing really well with that until New Year's Eve. It had been four months since it had all begun and I missed my two friends. Knowing Cameron was still as raw as I was, I text Evan to wish him a happy New Year. I received no response. I don't know why, but that moment hit me very hard. I was crushed. I remember feeling like someone had just stabbed me in the stomach, and it was at that moment that something changed within me. I remember feeling that old feeling of rejection and betrayal, and suddenly screaming to myself, *ENOUGH!* I mentally pulled out the wounding dagger I had placed in my abdomen, looked down into the core of my being and yelled, *Ok, who is feeling this? What younger me is hurting right now?* I shouldn't have been surprised, but I was actually stunned when my eight-year-old Kelly raised her hand. *It's me.* She said. Eight years old was when I had realized I was speaking to someone from the other realm and eight years old was when I rejected my own clairvoyance, not wanting to be flakey in the eyes of others. Compassion filled my heart when I asked her, *why are you feeling so hurt.* She emotionally, with quite the dramatic flair I might add, said, *Evan doesn't love us!* For a moment, I sat in stillness, contemplating what she had just said within me. I realized that I had developed the belief that people could hurt, betray and reject me at eight years old after I rejected and betrayed myself. I am clairvoyant and at that age I rejected the authentic me feeling I was not accepted if anyone really knew. I could see my self-rejection clearly and feel what she was feeling. It was at that moment I saw that I couldn't possibly be in a complete state of self-love if one of my younger "mes" still existed with self-rejection. I proceeded to ethereally pull her toward me and from my heart to her heart, teach her that she could not be hurt if she realized she truly was radiant love. Although I was the one teaching her this idea on the surface, she already knew deep within her wise self. She told me she knew, hugged me and I could feel how much she needed my acceptance, support and understanding. She didn't need to look for love from anyone else, but I could see that she did need it from me. At that moment she, and

140

I, realized that love is just love. You don't hand it to someone and they don't hand it back to you. At that moment I learned that love is not an action, it is a state of being.

That was a profound moment for me, and my eight-year-old self. Although at the time I still hadn't heard from Evan, I could only thank him for delivering to me the ability to see what was still broken within me. Until you amass enough mistakes, successes, pain, joy and experiences around a lesson, you will not move through it. At that moment, I had amassed enough and Cameron and Evan were my teachers. From then on I let my golden light shine, which is my radiance of BEING love.

By becoming this golden light, I truly understood the ego, what it was teaching me, and that in an effort to satisfy the ego's need to be accepted and loved, I had forgotten that I just AM love. Understanding that at such a core level changed me so significantly and was what had moved me into the Spiritization phase of Fermentation.

In the Emerald Tablet, the reputed original writing about alchemy, it explains that moving into Spiritization is the hatching of a new state of consciousness. It is often marked by meaningful visions that end the dark night of the soul learning. Out of the Putrefaction phase comes the yellow wax, which seeps into your brain bringing about true enlightenment. As the oily ooze works to heal your deep wounded child-you, you are turning into a brilliant golden light.

Nothing was the same after that. Darth Vader showed his good side and then he experienced his death. I too experienced a death, a death of an old way of believing. We can think in our minds all we want that "I understand that I AM radiant love!" but until we heal our deep-rooted child-self and the karma we came to experience, we do not experience this profound shift. I felt like I had died, went through the birth canal and came out the other side fresh and radiant.

Over the next five months I received help from so many beautiful human souls as visions about how to bring my Guide's messages to the world flooded in. Doc Russ was one of the angels who came forward to help guide me in developing an online classroom where I teach people about these messages and the stages of alchemical healing. He was tireless in his devotion to do good for the world and help me create a forum without wanting compensation at all. Jonny and Dennis came forward to develop logos that inspire and heal others with the sacred geometry held in their designs. Kevin came forward to help me move more fully into the softer, gentle side of myself. Nia continued to provide an ear and shoulder and allowed me to stand fully in the bigness of my spirit. And Doc and Carol provided me with an amazing mountain home that further healed my spirit and allowed my new golden light to shine. I felt the universe bringing to me all of the assistance I needed to move from a soul experiencing learning to a soul who could now give back.

At this time of golden radiance you will find that life is easy, effortless and it feels like the very stars are conspiring to bring you all that you need. Your wisdom is capable of operating with clarity and without much triggering. Your soul is open to expansion and to new understandings and it is during this time that you can operate as the true wise being you authentically are.

One of the most beautiful understandings that occurred at this time was experiencing living life AS love, not looking for it. When you experience life as love it is difficult to take things personally, to project onto someone else or to traverse down the mental rabbit hole when life gets a little tough. You learn to operate in a different way.

During this time I learned about evolved love. That March, at a Gregg Braden workshop in New Mexico, I met Kevin. Kevin was a bold, outgoing man with a huge zest for life. As an Australian, he was in America on a limited visa, but that didn't stop us from sharing our journey together for a short time. For a few months we just played, and I found I could easily radiate who I was in his presence. As none of us are, he is not perfect, so there were times that he showed up during our time together as hard and out of congruence with what I was radiating. The old me, prior to my Fermentation stage, would have pointed a finger, been a little self-righteous and schooled him on how unwise he was being. Instead, I was given the opportunity to stand outside of the situation, at every moment it got a little hard, and experience a softer, wiser me. I was able to not project at him, not point a finger, but look inside at what I was reacting to. Gary Zukav's latest book, "Spiritual Partnerships" speaks of our relationships evolving from friends to spiritual partners. In this wise, heartfelt book, he explains that spiritual partnerships have a willingness to explore their inner pain in a mutually beneficial way so as to promote each others' growth. His words speak volumes to me and during this time with Kevin, my Guides had me write a wisdom class around evolving love. I used some of what Gary taught, some of the personal experience I was gaining around this subject, and some of the teachings of my Guides.

My Guides taught me that evolved love has no expectations other than to expect that each of us is on our own personal journey. They are serious too, absolutely no other expectations. Our journey is ever changing, ever evolving and is personal to each of us. The moment that we expect something of anyone in our lives, including an intimate relationship, we are actually ruining the relationship. How can we place an expectation on someone if we respect their journey? That journey may cause them to be unfaithful, hurtful, inattentive, ignorant, or display a whole plethora of different human-journey behaviors you may not like. People do this because they are busy playing out the karma they need to so that they can heal through what they came here to learn. The only thing you can expect is that they will be on their journey regardless of what you say or do. Now, before you give me a *Sister please! Let me tell you a thing or two about relationships!* finger shake, let me explain a little further. We all have desires for who we want to attract into our lives. I personally want to attract into my life someone who is spiritually evolved, kind, loving, playful, healthy and is as interested in continuously learning to be a more beautiful soul having a human experience as I am. But I cannot expect that they will be that. I can desire it only. Once I am in a relationship, all I can do is observe. If I observe something that is not congruent with what I desire, I can then take a step back, look inside first, process my own feelings, ask why that bothered me and then seek to engage in a conversation with whomever I am in a relationship with. By the way, this approach includes all human relationships—family, coworkers, lovers, friends, etc. Regardless of who you are seeking to engage in conversation with, the conversation is not about them. The only thing you can talk to them about is your experience inside of you and then listen should they wish to share their own internal experience.

Should there be something you observe in another that either upsets you, saddens you, or bothers you, all you can do is share your feelings, placing no focus on them. The conversation might go something like this. "So...remember when you said you thought I was just like my mother. I am going to share how that sat with me. I cannot presume what you meant; and I want you to know that whatever it is that you meant is not for me to judge, own or change. What I am going to share with you is how I felt about it, what I went though inside of me. Can we just start a conversation around this?" This conversation is not manipulative, projecting or judgmental. You are only seeking to speak your own personal truth and genuinely seek to hear theirs. This is your opportunity to own your feelings and not make someone else responsible for them. Through my experience with Kevin, I was able to explore these types of conversations and see how much more healing and effective they are for everyone involved.

In my classes and in my sessions with clients I talked about these types of conversations often and found that, for many people, the tricky part is when you are in a relationship where the other person cannot hold these types of conversations. It is at this time that what you observe in another is perhaps not in alignment with you. I tell my students and clients that it is not for you to judge

145

or reject, just ask yourself if this is something you can exist with. If you cannot or do not care to exist with someone who cannot hold these types of conversations, you let them go with love for who they are and what they are learning here. You are still loving their journey unconditionally; you just choose to not have what they are learning about in your intimate space. I say often, I don't like when someone hurts others, but I have no right to judge them for how and what they are learning on their journey. If you realize that someone is just not a match for your journey, you don't have to tell them they suck as a spiritual partner, or tell them they are just not evolved enough, that is really just superiority and comes from ego. Don't make drama around it or have a big parting of the ways if you don't need to. Just let the relationship fade naturally if you can. It is quite typical for old, unhealthy relationships to naturally fade at this stage of alchemical change. Consequently, you draw to you new, healthier, more balanced relationships that are at a similar stage of evolvement as you.

During this phase of Spiritization, or golden radiance, you learn to view life from within first. Whatever is happening outside of you is brought through a filter of the center of your internal golden light. Because of that you are continuously aware of your own feelings and reactions, without judgment of others or projection on to them. Prior to moving into Spiritization, I would use a phrase like, "You hurt me," which was nothing more than my projecting my own internal, personal wounded self onto someone else. They didn't hurt me. Well, their actions might have felt bad to experience, but the only one who can hurt you is you. Someone else's action may be the trigger, but the hurt is self-created. When you tell someone else that they

146

hurt you, it is like you are taking your own internal strength and handing it over to them saying, "Here, I give all the power of my internal being to you. You have the power to dictate how I feel and how I respond, and what I think of myself as a result, so here is my power, it is yours."

A Note on Evolvement

For the sake of this book, to evolve means to grow as a being by allowing yourself to take gradual steps toward changing your opinions or beliefs about yourself, humanity, life and existence. What you are evolving toward is shedding the control of the ego to realize that you ARE love.

These changes in opinions and beliefs gradually bring you into a happier, healthier, more self-loving you. In the alchemical process, we are learning about all levels simultaneously, bit by bit, and we are all continuously evolving at our own unique pace. So often in the spiritual development world, the word evolvement is used in context with the ego. When used in this context, stating that you are more evolved often comes across as a level of status, which is nothing more than ego exemplified.

Are there levels of evolvement? Of course, however, it should never be used as a status symbol. It is just an indication of where you are at in your studies. When the ego is removed from this lens, evolvement is simply a way of saying that one is progressing in their studies as a soul having a human experience.

All levels of growth are beautiful. A baby soul can grow (evolve) more in a lifetime than an old soul, which does not place them in any hierarchy. Evolvement should be viewed as an indication of learning, not a level of status to be reached.

During this Fermentation stage, there is so much that is learned about love because you are finally in a space of genuine self-love that comes from understanding that you just ARE love. As my Guides explain, love is just love. From the way that they look at it, there is not one kind of love for your mom, another for your brother, another for your best friend, another for your dog and yet another for your partner. Love is just love. It is the ego that wants to put conditions on love. Sexuality and sexual attraction is different. During this time of understanding the true nature of love, you will see the difference and come to appreciate how magical it is when there is genuine love and sexual attraction together, but regardless, love is just love. Anything else is based in the needs of the ego.

As I was learning about the true nature of love, I was continuing to write weekly wisdom classes, trainings and workbooks that contained life-long teachings, presented by my Guides. I continued to deliver private sessions with people, helping them to heal their younger "thems" and find their own self-love. With every session my Guides would take me deeper into the healing my clients were experiencing and I learned more and more about how to help others grow and transform every day. It was such a beautiful time of being in such a peaceful space within myself. I had moved through both stages of Fermentation; Putrefaction, or my dark night of betrayal and Spiritization, coming through the birth canal a new radiant being of love.

For this stage to present itself to you, allow your growth at every level, not resisting it with projection, resentment, or victimization if you are able. And should you find yourself in those places of projection, resentment or victimization, don't judge yourself. Remind yourself that you are human and you came here to learn all about not doing that by doing it. Just as you learn to love others unconditionally, embrace this unconditional love within yourself, too.

- Take the time to recognize the human conditioning you developed in Calcination
- Let go of the pain, wounding, self-judgment, and false beliefs about yourself in Dissolution
- Acknowledge when the Ego presents itself in you and call it out when it shows up in your life in Separation
- Desire to balance your opposites and see the value in both the masculine and feminine energies in Conjunction

Once this is experienced you will naturally Ferment. You will rot and ooze. Do not judge it. Keep with your higher self and even when you do explode with anger, project hurt onto another, feel wounded, feel victimized or resent, just know that it is all part of the process of letting go of the biggest thing your wounded inner child needs to let go of. This is kind of like taking a security blanket, a nook or a bottle away from a child. Your inner child will throw a temper tantrum, cry, resist, think the world is ending or feel wounded and sad, but it is all for the best and eventually that inner child will realize they are stronger and more capable once they let ego of the false beliefs they created about life. Your ego will try to keep your "pain blanket" fully present. It may throw a last tantrum, but stay the course with wisdom and compassion for all involved, including you, and you will move through the dark night of your soul into your new golden light.

After radiating my golden light and bringing through enlightened visions of the content for my online wisdom classes over the next five months, apparently my Guides decided it was time for this book. It was June 2016, when I had the vision I described in "the beginning" and I see now that they could not bring this book through me until I could radiate AS love, not as needing love. What is inside of a person is put into whatever they create, be it music, painting, acting, writing or any form of expression. The energy of someone's creative expression moves into everyone who experiences viewing, hearing, or reading that expression. My expression of love is this book so I can see that for this book to heal and transform others, it needed to be coming from a place free of false beliefs of the ego.

After having the vision for this book and my Jonnyworld experience, I explained that Karal, my southern friend, had been staying with me for a couple of days. While I was busy having at least a four-hour, mind-blowing, holy cow experience in thirty minutes, Karal tried several times not to send me an email. She explained to me that while I was there she received a flier in her inbox about a Hay House Publishing workshop that was going to be held two weeks from then in Maui, Hawaii. She said that she was getting this hit to send it to me, but kept saying to herself, *Why do I want to send this to Kelly, she's not writing a book!* She tried three times to blow it off and not send it to me, but eventually just sent it. After I explained what happened and told her that I was going to be writing a book and going to Maui she told me of the email with the flier in my inbox.

False Beliefs of the Ego

When we come here to Earth to learn our lessons, we exist with an ego. The ego keeps you looking for love and acceptance outside of yourself and importance through the eyes of others. Because of this it is based in fear. Fear of not having enough, not being enough, not being accepted, or not being loved. The following are examples of the ego's false beliefs that can develop due to your own personal human conditioning.

- I am not good enough
- I am not smart enough
- I am not pretty enough
- Life is cruel and hard
- I can be rejected
- I am better than others
- I can be betrayed
- I need others to respect me
- Other people are better than me
- I need others to see me as important
- Power money and status define me
- My unique qualities are unacceptable
- I blame someone else for my miseryI need someone else to love me for me to be complete
- I need to control others or my surroundings to be safe or important
- I need people to understand, accept and acknowledge me
- There is a particular way to behave and live your life and if someone does not behave or live this way they are unacceptable

- I cannot control what happens in life
- I am a victim
- Life is unsafe
- My success defines me
- My belongings define me

Two weeks later I was packing for Hawaii. And two days before I was to leave my Guides said to me, *Pack everything up, end your lease and give away your belongings because you don't know when you'll be back.* As instructed, I let go of my belongings—crystals, art, clothing—the whole lot. What I owned now fit into a small suitcase and a backpack. Well, my skis, rock-climbing shoes, massage bed and tent are in storage, but aside from that my life now fit into what I could carry in my own two hands.

I did attend that workshop and I radiated as I wrote in Hawaii for twenty-two days. I felt complete as I explored the feelings of existing as love and hoped that time would never end. But, as we all know, the winds of change are always knocking at our door and they can either blow you over or blow you forward. I think my next change was a little of both.

I remember, while I was writing in Hawaii, saying to my Guides, *I don't know that I have experienced the Distillation stage yet. You will have to give me some guidance on that.* Damn. You know that saying, be careful what you wish for? Ugh. The words of Willy Wonka, "Scratch that...Reverse it" are ringing in my head, but there was no reversing my wish; experiencing Distillation was to come at me full force.

And to Canada I went.

Summary of the Fermentation Stage

- This is the stage of change
- There are two phases of change, Putrifaction, also known as the dark night of your soul and Spiritization, also known as shining your golden light
During the dark night of your soul you will expose the false beliefs your ego created based on your unique human conditioning
- Once you expose your false beliefs you have the opportunity to heal those deepest wounds of your child self
During the time of your dark night, resist creating a story around it and becoming a victim
- During the time of your dark night, resist judging yourself or others, look within for your growth and healing
See the perfection in all experiences, even when they are hard, and view them from a higher perspective
- Once you move through your dark night, radiate from within as pure love and let your golden light shine
Allow relationships in your life to exist without any expectations, only compassion for the journey each of us is experiencing
- Learn to live view life from within, bringing all experiences through your golden light before projecting out at anyone else
- Shine baby, shine!

Chapter Six
Distillation
Purification

*Acid burns...keep it out of your mouth and
your tongue won't spit fire*

*Your reaction is your lesson.
Your reaction to your own reaction is your
learning.*

Reminder of the Alchemical Stages

Stage 1: Calcination:
To convert with heat or burning (human conditioning)

Stage 2: Dissolution:
To undo or break down (heal internal wounding)

Stage 3: Separation:
Breaking apart or letting go (see the ego when it shows up)

Stage 4: Conjunction:
Union (balance your opposites)

Stage 5: Fermentation:
Change (Dark night of your soul and golden light)

Stage 6: Distillation:
Purification (let go of old habits and safety zones)

Stage 7: Coagulation:
To change into a thicker, stronger mass

Distillation, in chemical alchemy, is the boiling
and condensation of the fermented solution to
increase its concentration. It is a process where
any last remaining impurity is distilled off and the
purity of the substance is reached. Alchemists

155

believe that repeated distillation releases the essence or "spirit" of a substance. This repeated distillation produces an extremely concentrated solution through a process called sublimation, where solid matter turns directly into a gas. Through this process the vapors from the solid matter condense on the hood of the distillation apparatus and a white powder collects. The white powder is why this stage is often called the white stage of alchemy. This white powder is also what alchemists called the Mother of the Stone because it is what will give life to the final stone called the Greater Stone, or Philosopher's Stone.

Unbeknownst to me, my Guides were granting my wish to know more about this Distillation stage, though all I knew was that I was internally called to go to Canada to meet with a woman about my website, social media and to create a social platform for this book. Something in me was apprehensive about going, but I also knew I needed to go. I was about to experience the perils of Distillation and this would take me completely by surprise.

A woman, who I will call Birch, had exactly the talents and spiritual interest that I believed was needed to get my social platform developed, and to assist me in further developing my online wisdom class community. I was so excited about all that was promised and I wholeheartedly accepted the help that was being offered. Birch is an intelligent, twenty five year old woman who has a beautiful presence. She has many talents, which developed due to her tenacious spirit that told her nothing could stop her from learning about, or doing anything. We began working on a website and dreamed together of making the Inner Wisdom Circle an even more expanded community for like-minded souls. This was a very exciting time and it appeared to me that my golden light was just going to keep on shining. Well, that was partly true, shine it did, but there were still some impurities that needed to be distilled off of me. It was through the stage of Distillation that I learned of the power of personal, internal safety mechanisms. What I like to call our safety zones. My safety zone seemed to be marked off by orange cones and bright yellow tape that said, "Caution, Do not cross!"

Safety zones are reactionary behaviors we established during our Calcination stage that perceivably kept us safe in and against life. I had two safety zones that were prevalent in my life, one was my tendency to bolt when things were threatening and the other safety zone was my anger. Hence, my dad's saying, "There she goes! Stomp-stomp-wiggle-wiggle-slam!" My stomping off, wiggling my hips defiantly, was safety zone number one – the bolt. The slam was safety-zone number two, my feisty, anger. You may recall that in the Conjunction stage I explained that I used my anger as a defense against the "mean" life I thought I was living in. Subconsciously, I believed that if I stayed in anger and forced away anything I didn't like in life, I was safe and couldn't be hurt.

The human perception is that these safety zones serve us and in some ways they do. Mine served me so that I could survive my teen years, and in the Conjunction stage it helped me bring balance to my masculine and feminine energies. I am grateful for my anger as a teacher. However, as a self-loving, balanced being who wanted to keep shining her golden light, the old habits of resorting to either of these zones no longer served who I had become.

157

Birch's safety zone is control. There is no judgment about this; it is just what her safety zone is. If I judge her for having control as her zone, then I have to judge myself for having anger as mine, and frankly, that makes no sense to me at all. As I said, we all have these go-to safety-zones.

Safety Zone Examples

Safety zones are coping mechanisms, or go to behaviors, that we subconsciously believe keep us safe against life, ourselves or others. They are typically developed before the age of thirteen and may have authentically kept us safe in childhood. Although in adulthood these safety zones usually no longer serve us, they tend to stick around as a reactionary, habitual action we take because that is what we are accustomed to. They are our default behavior when things are perceived as difficult or unsafe around us.

- Drama
- Victimization
- Control
- Manipulation
- Narcissism
- Superiority
- Disassociation
- Running away
- Dismissive of others
- Rationalizing rightness
- Alcohol/drugs/food/sex
- Being the center of attention
- Knowing more than others around you
- Depression
- Giving away your voice
- Hiding internally
- Projection
- Avoidance
- Checking out of life
- Anger
- Logic
- Shouting

Since I had only planned to be in Canada a short time, Birch and I worked day in and day out. Our time together was extensive and living within Birch's control-zone eventually resulted in my engaging my anger-zone. I am very tolerant of others' behaviors because I understand why these behaviors are present within them, but despite my understanding why Birch had her control-zone I eventually reacted to it. My reacting resulted in my engaging my own safety-zone.

It took about seven weeks before I reacted, but react I did. And my anger started to show its need to distill off. It started with just a few little snippy comments here and there, like, "I think I know how to drive to the store, I've been doing it just fine for forty-eight years now." Oh yeah, that's snippy. In the process of Distillation, boiling and condensation of the fermented solution has to happen to make it a more concentrated, thicker mass. I had been given a concentrated dose of control and I had begun to boil for sure.

I must say, this stage came as quite the blow after radiating in such a loving space within my golden light. And, unfortunately, I didn't recognize my surfacing of anger as my Distillation stage until it was already at the boiling point. As I look back now, I am so surprised at how passively I allowed Birch's control zone to be in operation without being proactive in stopping it. But I also know that without my reaching my boiling point, my anger would not have had the opportunity to be distilled off. As I look back at this, I honestly don't regret a thing. I can see how perfect it was for me to blow. I smile as I think, *Oh, these stages of alchemy are little creepers! They creep up on you when you least expect it, immobilize you, hold you in their stare and say, "Well now, what are you going to do now?"*

What I did was I blew. Poor Birch didn't understand what was happening. She couldn't understand why I was upset because she couldn't see her own safety zone, only mine. When we are so accustomed to the habit of retreating to our safety zones, we just see it as a normal function of our life and it is typically unrealized how much it

159

affects others around us. My higher self knew why Birch's control-zone was present. I felt compassion for that, but as I said, my anger-zone ended up surfacing regardless. It surfaced because that was the habit I had been accustomed to retreating to in my past when I felt threatened in some way.

Over the next few days, I became more and more frustrated and began to outwardly get snappy, not just snippy. In my world, snippy is acting like a little dog with one of those little yippy barks that are irritating but really have no power behind it. But snappy is acting like a big dog with a big bark that commands attention. Well, my snips turned to snaps and that is when Birch also snapped. When she became frustrated back she became passively aggressive, and when she did that I became more frustrated and retreated further into my safety zone. Consequently, over the next couple of days, both of our safety zones increased as we both felt we were no longer safe from each others' reactions. It was a nasty little net that trapped us together as we each hit our boiling points.

In chemical alchemy, Distillation involves releasing volatile essences, from their prison in the matter, by heating it until it boils. This is precisely what had happened to me. The perfect trigger, Birch, was placed in my reality and consequently I boiled. This allowed my anger-zone to present itself, showing me that I had something that needed to be released from my behavioral habits.

Although we did not engage in outward fighting, we were pushing and pulling against each other and it was a very uncomfortable and unwanted scene for both of us. Imagine how uncomfortable it would feel to uncontrollably swear and yell at a

160

ceremonial honoring of Mother Theresa. Although I wasn't swearing and yelling, my almost uncontrollable snappy comments felt much the same.

I couldn't help but feel disappointed after coming as far as I had with my golden glow and I had to fight hard against self-judgment. I had to stop my mind from traversing down the mental rabbit hole, saying things like, *Have you learned nothing? What kind of a spiritual teacher are you? What are you doing, going backward in your growth? This is an epic failure!* I had to remind myself of what I often say to my students and clients,

> "Your reaction is your lesson.
> Your reaction to your own reaction is your learning."

What this means is that when we have a blow up, react in a not-so-nice way, or do something we wish we hadn't, it is not only about how you react externally that determines the level of your growth. It is equally as much about how you reacted to yourself internally about your external reaction. In other words, if you beat yourself up for how you reacted you are not only bringing your vibration into a lower state, but you are also making an internal statement that you don't accept that the human journey is full of mistakes.

Mistakes are absolutely necessary for you to move through the karma you chose to learn about in this human experience. Again, I'll remind you, until you play out enough mistakes, successes, failures, emotions, behaviors and experiences around a life lesson; you are not ready to learn it. In situations where you don't act in a way you feel is serving of your highest self or reflective of a wise, loving

161

person, it is important that you are understanding of and gentle with yourself. Understand that your reaction is only communicating to you that you still have something to learn, and be gentle with yourself as you engage in that learning. The measure of whether you have learned a lesson is two-fold; how you react externally and how you react to yourself and the situation internally.

Although it seemed like forever since my anger-zone had decided to figuratively punch Birch in the face, it had only been about a week, and then it was done.

My editor, friend and mutual teacher, Elizabeth had been visiting at the exact time the Birch-Kelly-Push-and-Pull-Safety-Zone-Match hit its high. This Elizabeth is not to be confused with my daughter Elisabeth, who is Elisabeth with an "s" she is Elizabeth with a "z". I believe her "z" stands for her beautiful zany, Zen-like nature. Well, lovely Ms. Zany-Zen witnessed this tense colliding of zones and was a bit surprised. She had really only known the wise, spiritual side of me. Yet to my equal surprise she did not judge. When you are in the line of work I am in it is way too easy for people to want to put you on a pedestal and make you their spiritual guru. They want to see you as flawless or unshakable and don't like to see you as human. There are some people who only want me as a spiritual teacher friend. Then there are those who accept me just as I am—human and fallible. Elizabeth is one of those people who I am honored to call my unconditionally, loving friend.

After witnessing my anger-zone she said to me, "It was so weird. When you got into the room with Birch you made yourself small and the anger came as such an immediate defense for you." That really

162

struck me. I had become small because internally my wise-me understood Birch, and I didn't want to have my anger affect her. But it surfaced regardless. That statement told me volumes about what was happening. Yes, I saw it then. I saw the perfection behind the orchestration of bringing someone into my life who could mirror to me what I still needed to heal, while I too was mirroring to Birch what she needed to heal.

You may recall how in the Conjunction stage, the fourth stage, the alchemist adds in acid to accelerate the conjunction reaction? As I explained earlier, in the Distillation stage the Alchemists purify the new element by removing the impurities that were added, such as the acid. Here I was in the Distillation stage and I needed my anger-acid that was used, and served me so well in the Conjunction stage, to now be distilled off.

At the time of Conjunction, I needed my anger-acid to surface in order to bring balance to my masculine and feminine energies. That was great and the job was done, but unfortunately the habit of that anger doesn't just go away on its own, it needs to be distilled off in the Distillation stage. Because I had gone through moving into my golden light and operating with a tamed, balanced ego I was in a really good place within, so guess what needed to happen? It was time to purify.

My anger-acid safety zone was not something I needed any longer, but it was an old, old habit that needed to present itself in an obvious manner so that I could see that it was still present in my habitual, reactionary behaviors.

163

This stage helped me to see that I had old programming still running. Distillation is a repeated separation and recombination of the different aspects of your personality. It is necessary to ensure that no impurities from the inflated ego are incorporated into the next and final stage of transformation, so what needs to be let go will become quite evident. As I said, my safety zone seemed to be marked off by orange cones and bright, yellow caution tape—it was extremely obvious. And it obviously was no longer a match for who I had become. Without self-judgment, without resentment, without reproach, I moved into a place of acceptance of what needed to happen. I needed to love what Birch presented to me, love the younger me who developed her safety zone, and let it be distilled off without a feeling of failure, resentment or shame.

I left Canada. And although I didn't particularly like the situation I was not upset that it happened. I realized that our partnering was not brought in to be permanent, but was brought in as a lesson and that lesson was perfect in its teaching.

I reflected on our exchange in the upcoming weeks and realized that it showed me not only that it had come in to teach me about this stage of Distillation, but it also came to show me that I had not accepted the human condition completely. Oh, mentally I knew all about this human life, what it is teaching us. I knew that we are here to learn lessons through the human condition but if I had understood that fully, my anger-zone would never have been as reactive as it was to Birch's control-zone. I realized that one of the greatest lessons taught within the Distillation stage is that of detachment.

To explain detachment, I often use an explanation of the story of the Bhagavad Gita. In this ancient Indian text, God incarnates as a man, named Krishna, on Earth. The Gita is the conversation between Krishna and Arjuna, a prince who has agreed to fight in a battle between his king's sons and cousins. In the story, Arjuna is distraught as he foresees the imminent death of his teacher, relatives, and friends. Due to this sentimentality, he throws down his bow and arrows and decides not to fight. This is the simplest way I can explain this very big text. Krishna tries to tell Arjuna that of course he should go fight, which, in turn, horrifies Arjuna. Krishna explains that everyone on that battlefield chose their path, their human experience and their lessons in this life. Those who chose to be maimed would be maimed; those who chose to be killed would be killed, just like those who chose to be the hero or helping friend would be just that. He creates a parallel to our life here in the human condition. This world is like a battlefield where we are all playing out our own karma and we need each other, and all of our failings and imperfections to allow it to come to fruition.

The way I explain detachment to my clients and students is that we need to respect the journey through life and what each person came here to learn on that journey. We need to detach from the pain, suffering or heartache that we experience here because not only did we choose that, we also need it for our growth. When something is going wrong in someone's life, it is not your responsibility to save them, fix their situation or enable them. You can be kind, compassionate and supportive, but if you realize that this life is presenting each individual their lessons, then you also realize that you have no right to do their homework for them. A good parent knows that doing homework for their child helps the child learn nothing. Well, it is the same thing in life. When I see a man homeless in the gutter, I do not feel sorry for him. I feel compassion that his lesson is such, but I allow him to continue to engage in his learning without feeling bad about it. Feeling bad about it not only sends negative energy his way but it is disrespecting the journey that he chose to engage in. Now, if the homeless man took initiative and asked me to help him get out of the gutter, and was showing earnest efforts to help himself, then I would extend my kindness and ask what I could do to help. And if I did that I would continue to only take steps that were not enabling, taking control or leading him away from the lessons he came here to learn. I am disassociated from other people's life's lessons in the manner that I have compassion for each person's journey, even when it shows up punching me in the face. I may not like it, but I don't want to judge it, feel bad about it, or stop it from playing itself out as a karmic lesson for myself or anyone else.

Detachment from the suffering of life is not heartless, cruel or narcissistic. It is detaching from sentimentality that comes from a lack of understanding the meaning of our existence here. Remember, the Phoenix purposefully burned herself so that she could rise up a new, radiant bird of light. We are the Phoenix who came to experience the perils of the human conditioning through the needs of the ego. In this stage we detach from the controls of our own ego, allowing us to detach fully from feeling distraught about life's sufferings.

During the Distillation stage the alchemists need the ferment, the product resulting from the

166

Fermentation stage, to harden into a stone before it can be made permanent. This final phase of Distillation is where the distilled vapor turns solid. This produces an extremely concentrated solution the alchemists called the "Mother of the Stone." This is where your soul will have distilled off both the behaviors that no longer serve and the last remnants of the Ego's control. You are now ready to birth a stronger, thicker you in the final stage of alchemy, Coagulation.

The Distillation stage showed me clearly what needed to be released from me and I was provided the perfect situation in which to do just that. I was able to release my safety zones and my attachment to the human condition.

After leaving Canada, I had gone back to California to regroup with my daughter, Elisabeth. She is such an easy person to regroup with, just letting me be me as I just let her be her. Although I was busy, reconnecting with friends, seeing clients and teaching online, it was an easy time. My body and soul needed this so that I could continue to grow into this new distilled version of me. Again, I was provided the perfect situation in which to integrate into my new alchemized state of being. Not a challenging environment like it was in Canada, but a space that was nurturing and light. In this harmonious state I could feel adjustments happening to me. But I also knew I was not done traveling and alchemizing. So I asked my Guides, *Alright. I know I'm not done alchemizing. I can also feel that I need to be in a place that exudes feminine energies to finish this book, so where in this world do you want me to be?* And I went about my day. About an hour later I heard very clearly, "Belize" I stopped in my tracks, and with wonderment to no one in particular I said, *Belize? Where the hell is Belize?*

Summary of the Distillation Stage

- This is the stage of purification
- During this stage, old programming from your Calcination stage, will surface to show you that you have habits that need to be released
- Recognize your safety zones, or coping mechanisms, and allow them to distill off
- Resist self-judgment as you learn to view your own reactions to hard experiences as your lessons
- Learn to detach from human suffering by seeing hard experiences as everyone's lessons that provide the context for learning

---

Chapter Seven
Coagulation
To create a stronger (thicker) mass

You are the Phoenix rising up out of her ash
You thrashed, you plucked, you preened
Seeking the love of your origin.
Inevitable surrender loosens the grip of
despair,
Revealing wings of radiant light
Fly phoenix, fly

The mark of evolvement in this life is not
achieving an out of body experience.
The focus is on having an in-body
experience,

Reminder of the Alchemical Stages
Stage 1: Calcination:
To convert with heat or burning (human conditioning)
Stage 2: Dissolution:
To undo or break down (heal internal wounding)
Stage 3: Separation:
Breaking apart or letting go (see the ego when it shows up)
Stage 4: Conjunction:
Union (balance your opposites)
Stage 5: Fermentation:
Change (Dark night of your soul and golden light)
Stage 6: Distillation:
Purification (let go of old habits and safety zones)
Stage 7: Coagulation:
To change into a thicker, stronger mass

---

while having your eyes open to what else is out there.

The seventh stage of alchemy, Coagulation, is where the lesser stone, The Mother of the Stone, becomes the greater stone, or the Philosopher's Stone. The Philosopher's Stone is said to be a transmuting agent that is highly sought out by alchemists because they believed it could instantly perfect any substance to which it was added. Hence, the alchemist's ability to turn lead into gold.

Coagulation is the alchemical process by which something congeals, or thickens. What happens is that, at the end of the Distillation stage, the alchemist has a white powder he scrapes from the hood of his distillation apparatus. He continues to increase the heat on the white powder until it turns first to yellow and then to an orange or citron color. He then increases the heat again until the powder turns red. This is called Pulvis Solaris, which means Powder of the Sun. This is also the color of the Phoenix as she flies again in her radiant beauty. In the fire, the red substance flows like wax, without smoking, flaming, or loss of substance. It is then time to thicken the material. This is achieved through a reduction in temperature great enough to crystallize or solidify the substance. As the heat dissipates, the matter moves to a cooler state and it congeals into a form. This is where the stone forms into a thicker, stronger stone, the final stage, which creates the Philosopher's stone.

Because you allow yourself to move through the other stages, you will then be in a state of learning to radiate. By this stage, the hard work will be done and you will have learned so much about life, yourself and others that the only thing left is to shake out your new wings and learn to fly again. This stage of Coagulation cannot be forced, as is the case with the other stages, it just unveils itself in perfect timing. Because the core wisdom of existing as love has been gained throughout the previous stages, this stage is more about feeling into the changes that have been made within and allowing them to blossom.

We are all unique beings and will radiate in our own original way, so I cannot give a prescription for how you will shine your new radiant you. I cannot teach any techniques that will help you in its development, but I can share my story of transformation to help you understand what takes place.

As you can see throughout this book, I have learned, very well, to listen to the direction of my Guides. And upon their direction, I went to Belize. Knowing I was going to write, I wanted to find a place of peaceful solitude. Almost as if it dropped in my lap, I found the perfect location; a little one-room shack on an Island called Virginia Caye. This Caye, which I embarrassingly learned is pronounced *key*, is situated inside of the Belize Barrier Reef, in the Caribbean Sea, toward the southern part of Belize. Aside from the caretakers of the Island, a very quiet couple who live on their sailboat, I was alone. Well, not really, I also shared the island with millions of biting no-see-um flies and a 120-pound pig named Piggy. Over the course of eleven days I wrote, swam, wrote, snorkeled, wrote, meditated, wrote, swatted flies, and more flies, and still more flies and wrote some more. I could feel that having this time with my silence and the cleansing waters of the Caribbean was changing me internally, I just didn't realize how much.

During this time I befriended my boat captain, Captain Bryan, who transported me to the mainland when I needed supplies and took me snorkeling when I got bored with being in my own silence. We were the same age, had both lived in California and we both had a free-spirited, unconventional nature that caused us to become immediate friends. At the end of my eleven days of island solitude, I felt that I was not yet done with Belize but my much appreciated, fly-ridden shack was already rented out to someone else. I contacted Bryan to see if he could take me to the mainland to find a more permanent place to stay. Bryan told me he was heading north up the Cayes on a multi-day trip to Sarteneja so couldn't bring me directly inland, but I could hitch a ride to an island called Tobacco Caye. He explained that from there I could catch a ride to the mainland because they have a water taxi that travels in from there. This was a perfect plan!

It took us only a couple of hours to reach our destination, leaving plenty of time for me to catch the boat ride to the mainland. September in the Cayes is slow season and many of the islands are left with a skeleton work crew and only a few people who reside on the island. There are about four hundred plus Cayes and most of them are so small they are either uninhabited or have only a handful of buildings on them. Tobacco Caye is one of these and was functioning with a handful of crew and a few residents. On this day, as we walked up onto the island, we were both struck by the crowd of people who were there. Belizean people are typically gentle, kind and welcoming people. This is not what met us on this day. If you've ever walked into a local hole-in-the-wall bar in a small Midwestern town you would have a high probability of finding that all heads would turn as they speculatively gave you the, *What the hell are you doing in our bar?* look. You would instantly know you had just invaded a space you were not invited into. Well, that about explains the looks, and vibe, we got when we walked up from the beach. It felt like we had just come upon an island of pirates and thieves and we were definitely not invited to join their party.

Testing the social waters, Bryan asked a couple of men, who looked like they should actually be crouching in a back alleyway somewhere, if the boat taxi was still going to the mainland. With a dismissive tone and complete disinterest in being a friendly Belizean, one of them gave an affirmative grunt. Bryan looked at me and said, "I am not leaving you here." To which I begged, "No, please do not leave me here!" And this started my seven day cruise up the Caribbean Sea on a sailboat with Captain Bryan, his two dogs, Kiki and Bolo, and the most pure energies I am sure I will ever experience.

Looking back I now see the perfection of that day. Without the vibe we had felt and the attitude those men presented to us I would have stayed on Tobacco Caye and would not have gone onto the sea with Bryan. Sailing can be a very internally reflective experience due to the amount of time methodically watching the water pass by and the lulling movement of the boat. Since my computer and phone almost immediately ran out of battery, I could not work and could not communicate with the outside world.

I am extremely sensitive to the energy around me—always feeling other's vibrations, intentions, and emotions. Even in the most quiet of places I can still sense an electrostatic noise coming off of most everything—people, trees, electronics, buildings, animals, everything. There, in the purity of the crystal blue waters, I was free from static, free from pressures to communicate, free from pressures to work. The stillness of this energy was a perfect condition for my transformation. .

Throughout the trip I continued to just BE with the wind and water, regrouping, laughing with Captain Bryan and Kiki and Bolo. I don't think I've ever been so free and relaxed. After seven days on the water, I landed on a northern island of Belize called, Ambergris Caye, while Bryan continued on to his destination of Sarteneja. Here I began socializing again. What a joyous time! I met so many beautiful people from all around the world and I played like an innocent child. I was so close to finishing this book and yet my instincts and my Guides were telling me to take a break. During this time I assimilated back into interacting with people and it is then that I realized what had transformed inside of me.

In the Emerald Tablet, it is explained that within the Distillation stage the soul comes into balance with the Earthly being, bringing a conscious merging of the soul and body, while still having the human experience. It writes, "It rises from Earth to Heaven and descends again to Earth." In other words, within the Fermentation stage of radiating your golden light you will transcend the veils of this Earthly life, while in a body. You will then bring that knowledge and way of being back into Earthly life in the Distillation stage. By doing this you will marry soul and body. This will allow you to move into a harmonious existence of peace and wellbeing on all levels. That peace of existence will bond to your personality. This boding takes place because you have already done the work in the other stages and in this stage you learn to soar with joy, radiance and compassion because the wisdom you have gained is a part of you. When this happens you will raise your ability to function with a tamed ego to the highest-level possible, free from sentimentality and emotions and a need for personal identity. This is precisely what happened to me.

Yes, I am sure your first response is something like, "What? Free from sentimentality and emotions? How loving is that? Bear with me as I help you to understand that it is actually the most loving state one can be in. You see, there is a big difference between feelings and emotions. Emotions are physical and instinctual and are lower level reactions to what is happening in your world. Feelings are responses to your emotions and are influenced not by instinct, but by personal experience, and beliefs. You can look at emotions as being reactionary and feelings as different states of being based on the level of wisdom you have obtained. Think of it like this. Imagine that your significant other accuses you of doing something that you absolutely wouldn't do. A reaction would happen if you triggered in some way emotionally, like you were outraged, horrified, insulted, or maybe even hurt. This happens because your Ego still believes it can be hurt or insulted because it is still looking for acceptance and love outside of yourself. Or it might be that it is looking for importance in the form of being right or respected. However, if your wisdom tells you that any projection onto you has nothing to do with you,

175

you will know at the core of your being that you cannot be hurt by someone else. Oh, it may look like it, smell like it or maybe even taste like it has to do with you, but anyone who is projecting onto another person through criticism, blame, judgment, and so on, is really only projecting their own hurt and internal wounding onto someone else. Further, if you are in your wisdom, you are not looking to them for love, acceptance or importance because you don't need that from anyone else. You genuinely realize that love is not an action, it is a state of being, and you just ARE radiant love. What they think doesn't matter to your wellbeing or happiness and you can then view them with compassion.

When you are in a place of feeling as opposed to emoting, and someone projects an accusation your way, you seek to help them understand you without an emotional reaction. You might feel an aversion to what your significant other is saying, however, there is no emotional charge around it. You might feel compassion for them in the situation because you see that they are hurting, but you don't feel a need to say anything about that. You would simply respond with a desire to clarify without an expectation of the result. You might say something like, "I'm sorry you feel that way. I can't tell you what to believe or how to feel, but I will share with you my perspective of the situation if it will be helpful." I am sure that this sounds like a bunch of baloney babble, but I can honestly say that it is possible get to this point. One of the things that transformed in me is precisely this. It is like you are in observance of people and situations as opposed to having a reaction to them. You don't take things personally, and you are no longer in need of being right, validated or understood.

When you are free from emotions, you have feelings like compassion, awareness that you have an aversion to something, gratitude or joy, but you don't emote much. You are even and balanced in your temperament inside and out. When people show up in your life who are emoting, you are in quiet observance and realize you don't need to react to it. You enjoy life and become joyous about different experiences, people and places, but you don't become elated or sentimental. Elation is being overly joyous and sentimentality means excessive tenderness, sadness or nostalgia, and those extremes of belief and emotion are no longer present in the personality. In other words, you don't have extreme highs and lows emotionally.

My daughter, Elisabeth, was challenging me on this explanation of non-emoting when I told her it was happening to me. She said, understandably so, "I don't know that I want that to happen to me. I like having an emotional reaction to things. I think emotions are beautiful." I explained to her that not having an emotional trigger, positive or negative, actually leaves more room for feeling compassion and joy because human conditioning is not driving what you are feeling. I also explained that if you are going to get that high in excitement, you are also going to get equally that low with disappointment or sadness. When you are in a place of feeling as opposed to emoting you rein in the extremes and feel more balanced. You are not numb to life; it is quite the opposite. You feel alive and radiant; it just does not come from a place of ego reaction.

I remember the day I realized what it felt like to not emote. In the past, after moving through the Separation stage, I had learned to use my wisdom to quickly shift so that I did not have much of a reaction to negative experiences. But what I noticed (as I began to interact with people regularly again) is that when negative experiences came in, I didn't have to consciously think about moving into my wisdom. It just happened naturally. This told me that my wisdom had integrated with my personality and just became a state of being. When hard experiences came in, I was just calm and would sometimes even laugh about the situation internally. I also realized that it was not just with negative situations that I was not emoting, it was with the positive ones as well. I felt happy, joyous or radiant, but there wasn't much action with it. I just stayed pretty calm, radiating happiness from the inside of me, rather than through actions on the outside. That seemed to be what others were experiencing of me as well. I began getting constant comments about how happy I looked. People would say things like, "You're just beaming!" or "Your energy is infectious!" I became uninhibited in my personality, and just loved existing without any expectation of my day. I danced, smiled a lot, sang, played and radiated.

This is not the only change I noticed. Earlier I explained that in the Distillation stage peacefulness of existence bonds to your personality. When this happens, you will raise your ability to function with a tamed ego to the highest-level possible, free from sentimentality and emotions and a need for personal identity. Personal identity is situated in the ego. If you look at the definition of "identification" you would see that all explanations are based on someone viewing you from the outside. In this stage you shine and exist from the inside out and it just doesn't matter if someone else approves of, values, accepts or respects who you are from the outside. What they think no longer matters. If they judge you, you don't take it personally. You are not looking to them for love, acceptance or self-importance. Therefore, your personal identity no longer matters. It's not that you don't know who you are; you know that you are love. You know you have gifts and talents and they are free to express themselves in an unobstructed way. You will be uniquely you, so you have an internal identity in that you have personal characteristics. But it makes no difference to you whether or not anyone else acknowledges them. In this stage you will no longer need to be right, validated, respected, honored, accepted, seen, understood or justified by others. You will want to always continue to do your best, be kind and compassionate and consider others' feelings; however this is motivated from a place inside of yourself, not because of what is happening outside of you or how you look to others.

By distilling off your behaviors and habits that no longer serve you, your state of being becomes the most loving state you can be in. Because here on Earth we are still encumbered with the ego we don't get rid of the ego, we tame it by moving through our lessons in the other stages of alchemy. Remember that the ego part of you needs to be valued, loved, and accepted by others and seen as important in the eyes of others. That will no longer matter to you by the time you reach this stage. You will only see yourself as a beautiful soul having a human experience. Consequently, you won't want to see anyone outside of yourself as anything but equally as beautiful. And if they show up not so beautiful, you are in observance of that, not judging them.

After being on Ambergris Caye for about a month, I took a trip to Wisconsin to see my family and old friends. While there I ended up reconnecting with Evan, Cameron's twin. If you remember, Evan helped me discover that I could not be rejected, hurt or unloved by rejecting me. His not speaking to me helped me to truly understand that I AM love. Although I appreciated this, I was not so eager to see him. Just because I appreciate a lesson someone delivers, it doesn't make me necessarily want to engage with them. That was the case here; I appreciated the lesson; I just didn't like Evan's method of delivery. Well, through unintended circumstances Evan ended up at the same function I was at. We talked openly about what had happened with Cameron. Without emotion I spoke a non-judgmental truth about the experience. Evan would again set the stage for my growth, however this time it was on the positive side. He shared with me how much he had missed me and asked if we could hang out one night while I was here and reconnect. I agreed. On that night I was able to experience being in observance in a way I have never done before. As I was sitting talking with Evan, I realized that our past friendship came out of need. In this place of observance I was able to reflect without emotion on our friendship and realized that at that time I needed a friend and I needed his love and acceptance. I was never conscious of that until this moment. As I sat talking to him I consciously realized that I was in observance of him as a person. This may seem like something we all do, we observe those who interact with us, but this was different. When we observe people with our human conditioning in the driver's seat, that observance is coupled with the needs of the ego. I realized at this moment that the ego was not engaged and I actually remember consciously asking myself, *Hmmm...do I actually like Evan?* I felt into the question and realized that, yes, I did genuinely like him. I liked his personality, his caring nature and that I did indeed want to interact with him. I didn't need to be accepted by him, loved by him or understood by him; I just wanted to radiate as a loving person next to him and let him be himself next to me. No expectations.

I have since returned to Belize and I have seen this observance show up consistently in my life. It is part of the non-emoting and lack of need for personal identity because there is a lack of ego need.

So here I sit, detached from the human experience - not expecting anything from anyone or anything, not emoting - just feeling balanced and in observance of life in each moment it presents itself. I have a quiet confidence that allows me to radiate from within not caring whether anyone notices. I feel uninhibited in how I show up in life and feel like I have reclaimed an internal innocence that was once clouded by the need for ego importance. I see so clearly what this last stage of alchemy is all about: this is the moment when the Phoenix flies. She burns herself in Coagulation, picks herself up in Dissolution, observes her ego reflection in Separation, balances her footing in Conjunction, births a new her and radiates a new passionate fire from within her in Fermentation, shakes the dust off of her new radiant coat in Distillation and now it is time to fly.

In this stage you fly, not in a boastful or "see me" way, but in a way that allows your inner light to radiate outward with compassion. I have noticed that people either love you or hate you; are drawn to your light or are resentful that you get to shine it. In this stage the three treasures of Taoism—compassion, humility and moderation—govern your existence. You are moderate in what you do, not in extremes of anything, you are humble in your light and have compassion for everyone's journey, even when they are resentful of who you are.

Many have interpreted this stage of alchemy to be the stage where you can get to the point of Zen-like existence and focus on things such as out of body experiences. My Guides have said the focus is not on out of body experiences, it is an in-body experience. This stage is where you can live the human experience with conscious awareness of the purpose of your journey here on Earth. It is not necessarily about becoming so evolved and pure that you are then supposed to be a guru meditating all day long. This is the stage where you can live as a human, open to your intuition, from a place of love within and inspire others as you radiate and fly. You are a participant in this life, not above it. You are free to express your personal bliss and share your experience with others, which may inspire them to do the same.

This stage is living with a reality of what spirituality is. Spirituality is not necessarily sitting cross-legged on the top of a mountain, free from life. It is existing in the midst of the chaos of life while understanding the truths of the beauty of it all. It is witnessing the ego, human conditioning, emotions and our human evolvement with eyes open to its perfection.

It is seeing the drama of life play itself out without making it a tragedy.

Summary of the Coagulation Stage

- This is the stage where you become a stronger, thicker, wiser you
- You learn to be in observance of life and others
- You will acknowledge the truly beautiful soul you are who is gratefully participating in this human experience
- You will move away from reactionary emotions toward feelings based on wisdom and your temperament will be come even and calm
- You will have an authentic compassion for the human experience and all of the journeys we are all engaging in while here and beyond
- You will fly as the radiant, internally powerful Phoenix free from the constraints of the ego
- Your personality will reflect a merging of the earthly you and your soul you and you will inspire and motivate others to radiate as you do

Conclusion

The Emerald Tablet explains that moving through these stages is like an androgynous youth emerging from an open grave. You are neither masculine nor feminine in your approach to life; you are balanced with both. You are even in your temperament and are resurrected as a human who has been brought back to the innocence of your soul. You are in this state because you have been burned by the human conditioning in the Calcination stage. You have allowed yourself to let go of old false beliefs and pain in the Dissolution stage moving into a place of forgiveness and the beginnings of self-love. You've recognized the ego as it has shown up in your life and began to separate yourself from its vice in the Separation stage. You have balanced your masculine and feminine energies in the Conjunction stage, which in turn brought balance to your other opposite ways of existing. You entered the dark night of your soul in the Fermentation stage so that you could shine your radiant golden light. This led you to distill off old habits of behavior that no longer served you in the Distillation stage. And all of this led you to congeal into a stronger, thicker, wiser and more brilliant you in the Coagulation stage, where the transformation becomes permanent.

Just as once you have solidified your understanding that one plus one equals two, you don't slip backward and suddenly believe the answer is three. Well, you don't slip backward in your wisdom either. Once you allow these changes to solidify in you and your wisdom to replace reactions, this way of being and thinking is always available to you in a state of consciousness. Will you have challenges in your life, people who show up hard, or ups and downs in life? Of course you will, you're human. But the way in which you move through life is permanently changed. Challenges become easy, or easier depending on your perspective. You no longer are entangled with the ego because the goal of the ego—to seek love, acceptance and importance outside of yourself—is no longer your goal.

Perhaps you are already to this state, or perhaps you are at the beginning. Either way, the approach to all in life, whether it is living as the new androgynous youth with eyes wide open to the human journey or taking your first step toward healing, the answers you are seeking are never outside of you. All of your healing, experiences, relationships and achievements are being created from within. The Phoenix doesn't burn someone else to a white ash. She doesn't make it her responsibility to tell them all about their faults. And she does not fly for them. She moves through this process internally so that her external existence is radiant. She may have people, books, workshops or experiences that motivate her in her growth, or facilitate healing for her, but the work is hers internally. She changed because she chose to change.

So fly Phoenix, fly, and may we smile at each other's radiance and glory in the heavens of this earth and beyond.

You are the Phoenix.

You choose with conscious intent to pluck from yourself the plumes of innocence and brandish the flesh of fire.

With the qualities of the devil and Earth as your lair,

You strip yourself of the knowledge of flight.

You walk blindly into the flames of hell.

You face hell's demons as fear pulverizes and pride burns.

The conditions of battle burn you to shameful ash.

Finding courage, you stand with truth as your sword.

You battle.

One by one you call the demons by name and release yourself from their relentless grip.

Finding new footing, you balance your stance as you gaze at the battleground that surrounds you.

You feel victory, yet not the win.

Exhausted, you seek sleep, but find no rest,

For the bed you have to lie in is threatened by the nightmare of your final opponent

Thrashing and wailing, you walk through your darkest night, seeking to roust the devil himself from its stench and rot.

As it rears its ugly head it reveals,

it is but an infant crying loudly to be fed.

The disquieted predator that has so long
imprisoned you in battle,

Is you.

You extend a trembling hand, comforting its dark
cries

Nourishing it with compassion.

A golden radiance emerges, born of internal
alliance.

Comforting the child within,

You bow to the battlefield.

You honor the heroes, the cowards, the mystics
and cheats.

You relinquish your sword, and shake off the dust
of battle.

As you gaze above, you call the cry of the Phoenix

And spread your wings of new found radiance.

Fly my Phoenix, fly.

Epilogue

Although we have come to the end of the explanation of the alchemical process, our work is not done. Our growth never ends here on this earth. But it certainly does get easier!

We do not know what will come next after this internal growth and expansion, but we know we cannot go backward in our wisdom. We will continue to have our challenges and will continue to see life reflecting in our moods, our emotional charges, our radiance and our need for further growth. We welcome all of that for we have truly come to feel such appreciation for all of life's beauty. As we move through the alchemical process, we know that challenges and growth are not failure; they are perfect and are what will bring us further and further into expanded happiness.

As I stated in the beginning, there is another book in the making, which explains how to heal your physical body through inner alchemy.

I shared that I have had nine different health conditions and eleven different operations. After my last operation on my hip, I knew I was done with being a victim to my illnesses. I used self-love, Reiki and working at a molecular level to rearrange my physical body into health. All of my old health conditions are gone and although I should be in pain from bones and tissue being removed, broken, torn or displaced, I have none.

Look for this story in my next book, <u>The Art of Healing Your Physical Body Through Inner Alchemy</u>, and learn how, by healing your emotional and mental bodies, you have already begun your journey of physical healing.

About the Author

Kelly Schwegel has earned an undergraduate degree in education, a master's degree in Educational Administration and an educational specialist degree in Educational Leadership bringing her certifications in teaching, principal, director of special education and superintendent.

After working in the field of education for twenty years, she left education to follow her calling to train, speak and heal in the area of spirituality and the natural healing arts. She became a Reiki Master Instructor in 2011 and has taught countless individuals to heal themselves and guide others along their own personal healing journey.

Kelly has a passion for public speaking, and she instructs weekly through her online learning community, The Inner Wisdom Circle. She continues to take private phone clients as often as she can, helping others move through the alchemical growth process.

Kelly's family includes her daughter Elisabeth and her cat Charlotte. She currently lives in Belize where the waters are warm, the breeze is light and life flows slowly and freely.

Resources

Braden, Gregg. "Oneness and the Quantum Hologram." Spirit of Ma'at n.d.: n. pag. Print. Vol 3, No 12

Cross section image of a brain. Digital image. Shutterstock. Alexilus Medical, n.d. Web. Nov. 2016. <www.shutterstock.com>. ID: 113804242

Cross Section of Brain. Digital image. Dreamstime.com. Legger, n.d. Web. Nov. 2016. ID 60816752

Fisher, Dr. Bruce S., Drdr. The Emerald Tablet An Interpretation. Prescott: Subru Publications, 1996. Print.

Grammar rock. American Broadcasting Co., 1997. CD. "Conjunction Junction" used by permission from American Broadcasting Music, Inc. All rights reserved.

Hampton, Debbie. "What's The Difference Between Feelings And Emotions?" The Best Brain Possible. N.p., n.d. Web. Nov. 2016. <thebestbrainpossible.com>

Hauck, Dennis William. "The Azoth Ritual." Church of the Emerald Tablet. N.p., n.d. Web. 18 Sept. 2016. http://azothalchemy.org

Hauck, Dennis William. Alchemy Workbook. N.p.: n.p., n.d. Print. www.DWHauck.com

Hauck, Dennis William. The Secret of the Emerald Tablet Selections on the Emerald Tablet from Die Alchimie by Dr. Gottlieb Latz translated by Dennis William Hauck. N.p.: Athanor , 2005. Print.

Hawking, Stephen. A brief history of time: from the big bang to black holes. Toronto: Bantam , 1988. Print.

Hawkins, David. Power vs. force. Carlsbad, CA: Hay House, 2002. Prin

"Home." HeartMath Institute. N.p., n.d. Web. 24 Dec. 2016.

Latz, Gottlieb. Secret of the emerald tablet. Place of publication not identified: Holmes Pub Group Llc, 2001. Print.

Nouwens, Hein. Human skull/vintage illustration from Meyers Conversations-Lexikon. Digital image. Shutterstock. N.p., n.d. Web. Nov. 2016. <www.shutterstock.com>. ID: 96036

Waite, A. E. "COLLECTANEA CHEMICA." Sacred Texts. London, J. Elliot and Co., Oct. 2007. Web. Oct. 2016. <http://www.sacred-texts.com>.